**Cinema and Tec**

Steve Neale

# CINEMA AND TECHNOLOGY
## IMAGE, SOUND, COLOUR

© Steve Neale 1985
All rights reserved.
No part of this publication may be reproduced or transmitted, in any form or by any means, without permission.
First published in 1985 by
Macmillan Education Ltd, London and Basingstoke.
Companies and representatives throughout
the world.

Typesetting in Great Britain by
Type Generation Ltd, London
Printed in Hong Kong

British Library Cataloguing in Publication Data
Neale, Steve
Image, sound, colour
1. Moving-picture history — Technological innovations — History
I. Title
384'. 83    PN1995
ISBN 0–333–30122–6
ISBN 0–333–30123–4 Pbk

# Contents

| | |
|---|---|
| Page vii | **List of Illustrations** |
| Page xi | **Acknowledgements** |
| Page 1 | **Introduction** |

## Part One: The Cinematic Apparatus

| | |
|---|---|
| Page 7 | **1. Photography and the Illusion of Reality** |
| Page 29 | **2. Moving Pictures** |
| Page 41 | **3. The Invention of the Cinema** |

## Part Two: Sound

| | |
|---|---|
| Page 61 | **4. The Technology of Sound Recording** |
| Page 77 | **5. Sound and the Film Industry** |
| Page 91 | **6. Sound and Film Aesthetics** |

## Part Three: Colour

| | |
|---|---|
| Page 109 | **7. The Technology of Colour Photography** |
| Page 129 | **8. Technicolor** |
| Page 145 | **9. Colour and Film Aesthetics** |

| | |
|---|---|
| Page 159 | **Conclusion** |
| Page 161 | **Bibliography** |
| Page 165 | **Index** |

# List of Illustrations

| Page | |
|---|---|
| | **Introduction** |
| 2 | **Star Trek** (Robert Wise, 1979) |
| 3 | **Close Encounters of the Third Kind** (Steven Spielberg, 1977) |
| | **Chapter 1** |
| 11 | Engraving of a large camera obscura, shown with top and front cut away. |
| 12 | Da Vinci's first camera obscura |
| 13 | Transport of Saint Marcus (drawing of mosaic, XIIIth century). Venice, Basilica di S. Marco |
| 14 | The courtesan Morokouti of Echizen-ya with her child, and an attendant standing by. Isoda Koryusai, XVIIIth century |
| 15 | The courtesans Hitomoto and Tagasode. Kitao Masunobu, XVIIIth century |
| 15 | Courtesan leading a youth to her bed with a lighted taper whilst her young attendant sleeps. Harushige, XVIIIth century |
| 16 | Boy dancing with hobby-horse. Ishikawa Toyonobu, XVIIIth century |
| 17 | The Crucifixion. From the Psalter of Robert de Lisle. Before 1339 |
| 21 | The first daguerrotype camera, *c.* 1839. Made by Giroux |
| 22 | Talbot's early calotype |
| 24 | Phantasmagoria |
| 27 | Diorama |

## Chapter 2

33  Muybridge's horse in motion
34  Zoopraxiscope
35  Marey's photographic gun
36  Marey's chronophotographic image formed with man walking when photographed against a black wall, *c.* 1884
39  A mid-Victorian magic lantern show

## Chapter 3

42  Edison's kinetoscope
44  A Broadway kinetoscope
44  The Lumière Cinématographe, 1896
45  **La Sortie des usines Lumière à Lyon** (Louis Lumière, 1895)
46  **Le Goûter du bébé** (Louis Lumière, 1895)
51  **Shoeshine and the Barber Shop** (W. K. L. Dickson, 1894)

## Chapter 4

62  Edison Kinetophone
63  Amplifiers in place behind the screen
64  A sound on disc system
64  Edison's first sound apparatus
65  An earlier attempt at an amplification system
66  Cycle of operations in sound recording
66  Diagram of Lauste's sound recording camera, 1906
68  De Forest's phonofilm
70  Western Electric recording channel in operation
72  Vitaphone in operation
73  **Variety,** 7 August 1926, regarding Vitaphone

## Chapter 5

| | |
|---|---|
| 86 | Diagram of direct financial control of Hollywood |
| 86 | Diagram of indirect financial control of Hollywood |

## Chapter 6

| | |
|---|---|
| 101 | **Broadway Melody** (Harry Beaumont, 1929) |
| 102 | **The Congress Dances** (Erich Charell, 1931) |
| 103 | Gene Hackman in **The Conversation** (Francis Ford Coppola, 1974) |
| 104 | Gene Hackman in **The Conversation** (Francis Ford Coppola, 1974) |
| 106 | Laying the sound track for **Apocalypse Now** (Francis Ford Coppola, 1979) |

## Chapter 7

| | |
|---|---|
| 110 | Diagram of additive colour process, showing mixture of three primary colours producing white light |
| 115 | The Pathécolor Printing Room |
| 116 | Diagram of stencil-making machine |
| 121 | Diagram of shutter of Lee and Turner projector |
| 122 | Kinemacolor projector |

## Chapter 8

| | |
|---|---|
| 130 | Technicolor beam-splitter camera |
| 130 | Sectional diagram of an early Technicolor camera, c. 1920 |
| 134 | Diagram of three-colour subtractive system |

# Colour Illustrations

### Early examples of stencil colouring

From a series of epic Italian films on the life of Christ, *c.* 1909

From newsreel fashion sequences, *c* 1912

Two shots from **The Last Days of Pompeii** (Carmine Gallone/Amleto Palermi, 1926)

### Examples of tinting and toning

An arsonist at work, *c.* 1910. He enters a factory at night to set fire to it; as the flames flare up the shot is tinted red

The transition from night exterior to yellow-tinted lamplit interior has a similar effect, *c.* 1920

*c.* 1924. Chemical toning

*c.* 1924. The two techniques of tinting and toning combined to produce colour effects

### The Kinemacolor process

Black and white prints of **The Delhi Durbar** (1912)

A colour record of the above

### Technicolor

**Ben Hur** (Fred Niblo, 1925). One of the first films to be made using a two-colour subtractive process with a beam-splitting camera

Walt Disney's Silly Symphony **Flowers and Trees** (1931)

**Becky Sharp** (Rouben Mamoulian, 1935)

**Henry V** (Laurence Olivier, 1944)

**The Three Musketeers** (George Sidney, 1948)

**Black Narcissus** (Michael Powell/Emeric Pressburger, 1947)

**Across the Wide Missouri** (William Wellman, 1951)

### Eastman Color

**Kismet** (Vincente Minnelli, 1955)

# Acknowledgements

I would like to thank Ed Buscombe both for suggesting this project to me and for his constant editorial assistance, Roma Gibson for picture research and translations, and Linda Hopkins for her encouragement during the lengthy period it has taken me to research and write this book.

Stills are by courtesy of Brian Coe at the Kodak Museum, the Science Museum, the British Museum, the British Library, the International Museum of Photography at George Eastman House, the Stills Department of the National Film Archive, Bernard Howarth-Loomes, The Rank Organisation plc, Columbia Pictures Industries Inc., MGM–UA, Paramount Pictures Corporation, RKO, Walt Disney Productions, Francis Ford Coppola and United International Pictures. Cover stills are from *Live and Let Die* (© 1973 Danjag S.A. All rights reserved.), *Superman II* (© Film Export A.G. 1981. All rights reserved.) and *The Passenger* (MGM-UA).

# Introduction

It is the contention of this book that understanding the place of technology in the cinema requires not only a knowledge of science and of the production and evolution of machines. It is a question also of aesthetics, psychology, ideology and economics; of a set of conditions, effects and contexts which affect, and are in turn affected by, the technologies employed by the cinema. The existence of cinema is premised upon the existence of certain technologies, most of them developed during the course of industrialisation in Europe and America in the nineteenth century (photography, the camera, the projector, sound recording, the whole concept and practice of an art form dependent upon mechanical reproduction and mass distribution). However, cinema is not reducible to those technologies. Its effects, its processes, its development cannot be explained by their existence alone. Cinema is a complex phenomenon. It is an industry, and as such involves economic determinants. It is also, in Metz's words, a 'mental machinery', an apparatus for the production of meanings and pleasures, and as such involves aesthetic strategies and psychological processes.[1] Technology is involved at both these levels, as a necessary factor, but not as a sufficient cause or principle of explanation for either. Sound technology cannot explain of itself the ways in which its introduction and widespread and rapid adoption by the film industry led to a restructuring of that industry or to the prevalence of specific financial interests within it. Equally, the technology of various forms of colour cinematography cannot of itself explain why colour initially tended to be restricted in its use to genres and forms considered

1. See Christian Metz, 'The Imaginary Signifier', **Screen**, vol. 16, no. 2, Summer 1975

less 'realistic' than others (the musical, the costume spectacular, the cartoon and so on).

So, technology is a basic component of cinema, a condition of its existence and a continuing factor in its development (as witness, for instance, the importance of special effects technology in the recent and hugely successful wave of science-fiction films, from **Star Wars** on[2]). It has its own specificity, its own history: just as the economic, psychological and aesthetic factors involved in cinema cannot be reduced to the technology fundamental to them, so technology and its development cannot be reduced simply to the status of an effect produced by economic, psychological or aesthetic factors and processes. The history and current state of the cinema rather involve an uneven and often complex interweaving of all these elements, each conditioning, but not fully determining or explaining, the others.

The following chapters of this book seek to demonstrate that this is the case by discussing in context a number of the technologies that have featured prominently in the history of the cinema: photography and the visual toys and entertainments that preceded cinema proper; the camera, projector and other machinery basic to the existence of film; sound recording and reproduction; and, finally, colour. In each case I shall give an outline of the scientific and technical principles involved and then proceed from there to highlight and to discuss some of the economic, aesthetic and psychological contexts and effects entailed in the development and adoption of each particular

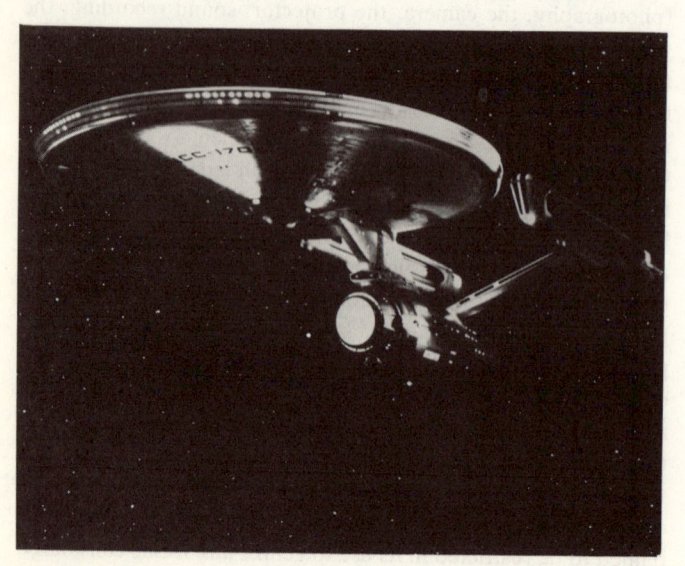

2. See Steve Neale, 'Hollywood Strikes Back – Special Effects in Recent American Cinema', **Screen,** vol. 21, no. 3, 1980

**Star Trek** (Robert Wise, 1979). *Courtesy United International Pictures*

**Close Encounters of the Third Kind** (Steven Spielberg, 1977). *Courtesy Columbia Pictures Industries Inc.*

technology. Above all, I shall attempt to focus on the ways in which these technologies can be seen to have had an impact upon the cinema considered both as an industry geared towards the production of profits, and as an institution geared towards the production of meaning and pleasure – towards the production of very specific forms of experience.

# Part One
# The Cinematic Apparatus

# 1:

## Photography and the Illusion of Reality

### Photography and Film

A strip of cine-film consists essentially of a series of still photographs which become animated during the process of projection and viewing. Photography is, therefore, in some form or another, a technical condition of the existence of film. One logical way of discussing it, and of viewing its historical place in relation to the cinema, would be to treat it simply as a stage in the ongoing development of film, a stepping-stone, an imperfect early version perhaps of what came to be invented some fifty years later.

An approach such as this, however, would miss the particularity of photography, subsuming it completely under the aesthetic and historical terms of the development of film. Moreover, in doing so it would, ironically enough, miss locating the particular role that photography *did* play in relation to the development of the cinema. As I shall go on to argue in more detail, photography was but one of a plethora of visual toys, entertainments and arts that came to pervade the culture of the industrialised countries during the nineteenth century, each of which contributed towards establishing a regime of visual representation whose existence was ideologically necessary for film and the cinema to happen. So the links between photography and film are ideological as well as technical. They have as much to do with the social role of vision during the nineteenth century as they do with the properties of silver halide.

In order to begin discussing these links, it is important first to examine some of the differences between photography and film, and in doing so to establish one of the particular features of the ideological terrain they each in their distinct ways occupy.

Empirically, the differences themselves are obvious enough: photographs are single, still images while films consist of a number of such images in motion; photographs register a moment in time while films register temporal sequences, and so on. But what are the implications of these differences? How, in particular, do they effect the relations between subject and object, viewer and viewed?

A photograph works so as to construct a representation which, on viewing, always becomes a representation and an evidence *of the past*. A photograph always says, in effect, 'this was'. The present time of the act of viewing is thus used, as it were, to confirm the existence and identity of the past. Hence the overwhelmingly nostalgic aura that many photographs tend to carry. Hence, too, their status as evidence.[1]

With film, the relations are different, due primarily to its extension in time and to the effect of presence that movement itself produces. If what has been filmed is perceived as having happened, in the past, duration and movement together ensure that there is nevertheless a much greater sense of the present time of viewing and of the present time of what is being viewed. You have only to freeze a film image and then set it in motion again to appreciate the difference. A photograph embalms the ghosts of the past; film brings them back to life.

This being the case, the two distinct modes of representation function quite differently in relation to subjectivity in general and to memory in particular; and memory, it is important to stress, is by no means simply a private, individual thing. In giving us our sense of ourselves as discrete, continuous identities, it performs an eminently *social* function.

In offering evidence of the past, photographs function as memory traces, as memories in and of themselves:

*A photograph is similar to a footprint or a deathmask. It is a trace of a set of instant appearances. The camera, like the eye, records appearances through the mediation of light. But the camera, unlike the eye, fixes the set of appearances which it records. If I look at you and then I look around, the appearances recorded by my eye are continually changing. What the camera does is to fix a set of appearances and, insofar as it does that, it is like memory. Memory preserves an event from being covered over and hidden by the events that come after it. It holds a single event. So does the camera.*[2]

Photographs memorialise the past. They remember for you. This is not to say that they are necessarily nostalgic. The memory they construct may not coincide with your own individual

---

1. As witness the themes of the discourse that surrounded them during the course of the nineteenth century: *Nobody who travels knows when he shall return. Therefore he ought to leave something behind for his friends to remember him by. What could be more appropriate than a Daguerrotype.* (Early advertisement, quoted in Gus Macdonald, **Camera** (London: Batsford, 1979) p. 14.) *A collection of these pictures may be made to furnish a pictorial history of life as it is lived by the owner, that will grow more valuable with every day that passes.* (Early Kodak advertisement, quoted in Helmut and Alison Gernsheim, **The History of Photography** (London: University Press, 1955) p. 302.) *I long to have such a memorial of every being dear to me in the world. It is not merely the likeness which is precious in such cases — but the association and sense of nearness involved in the thing ... the fact of the very shadow of the person lying there fixed forever!* (Elizabeth Barret, quoted in Susan Sontag, **Photography** (London: Allen Lane, 1978) p. 183.)

2. John Berger, 'Ways of Remembering', **Camerawork**, no. 10, July 1978, p. 1

history or experience. But they imply necessarily a difference between now on the one hand and then on the other. This distance shelters us from the reality we see, offering the position of an external viewpoint, but it also inscribes the loss that this distance involves, thus tending to engender nostalgia and to engage the psychological structures of mourning. Photographs provide an ease and exactitude of recall almost inconceivable before they were invented. The various genres of photography inscribe the balance between evidence and memory differently, as do particular practices within them. (Portraiture, for example, can in the family album function primarily as memory, while in police files it serves more overtly as a specific type of socially recognised evidence.) But its function overall is archival. It is no accident that the daguerreotype, an early form of photograph, was, indeed, nicknamed 'the mirror with a memory'.

Film, on the other hand, because of its temporal dimension, constructs and involves memory in different ways. It, too, is often overwhelmingly archival, but at the level of the viewing process itself, memory is differently engaged. Narrative has always played a crucial and fundamental role in the historical development of film, and one of the primary reasons for this is that it provides a means by which images can be sequenced and remembered coherently and easily. Narratives contain so much repetition that they enable the viewer to hold comfortably into a unity the duration of what has been viewed. Characters appear and reappear, the same locations recur across the length of a story, camera movements, colours, phrases and elements of décor are repeated so often that the process of the narrative is one in which forms of repetition are as fundamental as forms of difference and development.

From differences such as these one can begin to see that films and photographs operate in distinct ways, but that they nevertheless share a field of common concerns. Memory is one. And in both cases memory is related to vision and looking. Bearing this in mind, it is worth now taking a closer look at photography and its development and at a number of the characteristics it involves.

## The Invention of Photography

William Fox Talbot, one of the pioneers of photography, described the motivation behind his interest in the following terms:

*One of the first days in the month of October 1833, I was amusing myself on the lovely shores of Lake Como, in Italy, taking sketches from Wollaston's Camera Lucida, or rather I should say, attempting to take them; but with the smallest possible amount of success. For when the eye was removed from the prism – in which all looked beautiful – I found that the faithless pencil had only left traces on the paper melancholy to behold . . . I then thought of trying again a method which I had tried many years before . . . to take a Camera Obscura, and throw the image of the objects on a piece of transparent tracing paper laid upon a pane of glass in the focus of the instrument . . . It was during these thoughts that the idea occurred to me . . . how charming it would be if it were possible to cause these natural images to imprint themselves durably, and remain fixed upon the paper! And since, according to chemical writers, the nitrate of silver is a substance peculiarly sensitive to the action of light, I resolved to make a trial of it . . .*[3]

What is significant about this description is the conjunction of elements it assembles together: chemistry and optics, nature and art, memory and vision. What is also significant is the central place within it of the eye. It is precisely this central place that is at issue in photography as it has come to be institutionalised historically.

The basis of photography lies simply in the action of light upon specific compounds of silver, a process first studied scientifically by J.H. Schulze in 1727 and elaborated by C.W. Scheele in 1777. It is to this process that the word photography itself etymologically refers ('light-writing'). It is complete when the image produced is fixed on the base material used to support the compounds. This was first achieved by the Frenchman, Joseph Nicéphore Niepce in 1822 and subsequently modified by Louis Daguerre. As Hubert Damisch has pointed out – and as Alvin Langdon Coburn's 'Vortographs', Christian Schad's 'Shadowgraphs', Man Ray's 'Rayograms' and Moholoy-Nagy's 'Photograms' all demonstrate – this process in and of itself necessitates neither the camera (and its lens) nor the representation of objects, figures and scenes:

*Theoretically speaking, photography is nothing other than a process of recording, a technique of* inscribing, *in an emulsion of silver salts, a stable image generated by a ray of light. This definition, we note, neither assumes the use of a camera, nor does it imply that the image obtained is that of an object or scene from the external world.*[4]

Historically, however, the camera and the representations it produces have been crucial to photography, providing the

[3] Quoted in Brian Coe, **The Birth of Photography** (London: Ash & Grant, 1976) p. 22

[4] Hubert Damisch, 'Five Notes for a Phenomenology of the Photographic Image', October 5, p. 70

motivation for its invention and development and defining the parameters of its existence as a social phenomenon. As Fox Talbot's account implies, the chemistry of photography in a sense came last. What came first was the image produced by the camera, and the wish to register, stabilise and capture it.

Fox Talbot refers specifically to the camera lucida and the camera obscura as devices producing the kind of images which prompted him to wish to record them. The former, invented by Wollaston in 1807, was one of a plethora of camera-like devices invented and developed during the late eighteenth and early nineteenth centuries. The others included Charles's Solar Megascope (1780), Chrètien's Physionotrace (1790), and Varley's Graphic Telescope (1812), as well the Agatograph, the Digraph, the Eugraph, the Hyalograph, the Quareograph and the Pronopiograph. Each of these devices is evidence both of an intensification of interest and research in optics and of the refinement and proliferation of the system of representation and vision that they – along with the paintings and drawings they helped to construct – simultaneously enshrined and reproduced. Each, in turn, derives ultimately from the camera obscura, the other device Talbot mentions, and the one in which this particular system was initially automatically inscribed.

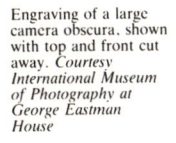

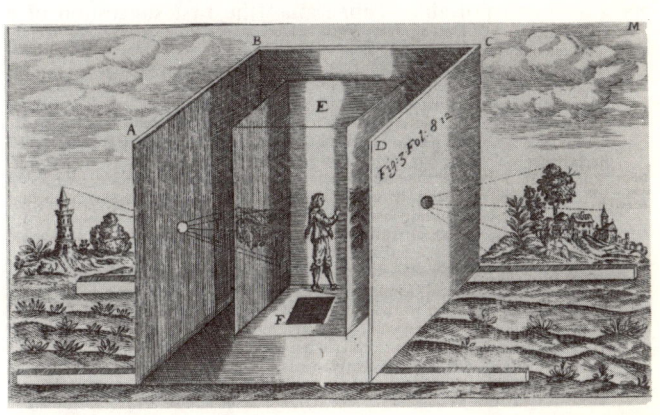

Engraving of a large camera obscura, shown with top and front cut away. *Courtesy International Museum of Photography at George Eastman House*

The camera obscura is basically a darkened room, cube or box with an aperture to let in the light. When the light passes through the aperture it produces an inverted image of the scene outside on the interior surface opposite. The image can be focused by placing a lens in the aperture, and the inverted image inverted again (turned the right way up, so to speak) by using a mirror. The basic principles of the camera obscura were first described by the Arab mathematician and scientist Alhazen in a ninth-century

Da Vinci's first camera obscura

treatise on optics. It was during the Renaissance in Europe, however, that it came first to be theorised fully (by the Dutch mathematician Gemma-Frisius in 1544 and by Giovanni Battista della Porta in his **Magiae Naturalis** in 1558; Alhazen's treatise was translated and published in Europe in 1572); to be consructed as a specific – and portable – apparatus (the first suggestion of a portable camera obscura was made by Friedrich Risner; the earliest reference to one occurs in Schott's **Magia Universalis** in 1657); and to be used in the production of visual representations (della Porta was the first to suggest that the camera obscura be used by artists and it was later clearly described by Leonardo da Vinci in his notebooks). In so doing it coincided with and reconfirmed the introduction and consolidation of monocular perspective as the system that was to transform the conventions of visual representation predominant in Europe up to the sixteenth century and to predominate, in its turn, for the next five hundred years.

The system was invented around 1420 by Filippo Brunelleschi and discussed in Alberti's treatise **On Painting** (1435). Prior to the use of the camera obscura, artists used a number of elaborate devices for making and calculating perspective. It was not until the camera obscura came to be used, however, that perspective came to be produced automatically. It is symptomatic that in his description of monocular perspective, Peter Pollack in **The Picture History of Photography** has recourse precisely to the metaphor not only of the camera but also of the projector:

5. Peter Pollack, **The Picture History of Photography** (New York: 1969) p. 19

*In inventing perspective, Brunelleschi envisaged himself as a kind of camera. He assumed that objects are perceived by means of a pyramid or cone of visual rays extending from the eye out into the world. His idea was to intercept this pyramid or cone by a plane, a short distance in front of the eye, in this way projecting the visual image on the surface of the plane just as a projector throws a picture on a screen.*[5]

## Perspective

Monocular perspective, as its name suggests, is based upon the centrality of the eye of the individual observer, a centrality marked theoretically in Leonardo's account:

*Perspective is nothing else than seeing a place [or objects] behind a pane of glass, quite transparent, on the surface of which the objects behind that glass are drawn. These can be traced in pyramids to the point in the eye, and these pyramids are intersected on the glass pane.*[6]

6. **The Literary Works of** *Leonardo da Vinci*, ed. J.P. Richter, London 1939, vol. 1, p. 150, cited in Stephen Heath, **'Narrative Space'**, Screen, vol. 17, no. 3, Autumn 1976, p. 80

It is marked literally in the description that Pollack goes on to give in his book of Brunelleschi's initial experiments:

*His first demonstration of the system was a small panel painting of the Baptistry of Florence made from inside the portal of the cathedral a short distance away. A sight hole was bored through the middle of the painting. Brunelleschi would put a friend at the standpoint from which the building had been drawn and have him*

Transport of Saint Marcus (drawing of mosaic, XIIIth century). Venice, Basilica di S. Marco

*sight the Baptistry through a hole in back of the painting. That done, he held up a mirror in front of the painting, blocking the actual view of the Baptistry but showing his friend a reflection of the painted view.*[7]

Monocular perspective differs from all other aesthetic and visual systems in constructing a rational and cubic space, and in regulating its co-ordinates as centring on a single point of vision. The space of Ancient Classical perspective is both heterogenous and discontinuous. Involving effects of relief and depth, Ancient Perspective is marked by the extent to which it refuses to unify them within an overall spatial framework.[8] The

7. Pollock, **The Picture History of Photography**, pp 19–20

8. Gisela Richter, **Perspective in Greek and Roman Art** (London: Phaidon, 1970)

The courtesan Morokouti of Echizen-ya with her child, and an attendant standing by. Isoda Koryusai, XVIIIth century. *Courtesy British Museum*

The courtesans Hitomoto and Tagasode. Kitao Masunobu. XVIIIth century. *Courtesy British Museum*

Courtesan leading a youth to her bed with a lighted taper whilst her young attendant sleeps. Harushige, XVIIIth century. *Courtesy British Museum*

space of Japanese art is centrifugal rather than centripetal. Its perspective effects function as a means of articulating a surface design rather than of erasing the presence of the surface in the interests of suggesting spatial depth.[9] The size and position of figures and objects in medieval art is governed by an ideological

9. See Noel Burch, **To the Distant Observer** (London: Scolar Press, 1979) pp. 91–2

Boy dancing with hobby-horse. Ishikawa Toyonobu, XVIIIth century. *Courtesy British Museum*

system rather than by their disposition within a cubic space. Individual viewpoints are scattered across the picture space rather than unified by it.[10] Space in monocular perspective is governed by the premise that light is propagated in straight lines and is both continuous and infinite and constructed from a single position. It is a homogeneous system constructed from a given point of origin – the human eye. It is the eye that is the point of coherence of the system.[11]

10. See Boris Uspensky, **The Semiotics of the Russian Icon** (Ghent: The Peter de Ridder Press, 1976) especially pp. 59–72 and 31–42

11. See Erwin Panofsky, **Renaissance and Renascences in Western Art** (New York: Harper & Row, 1972) pp. 122–7

The Crucifixion. From the Psalter of Robert de Lisle. Before 1339. *Courtesy British Museum*

These conventions, this system, was so strong, so pervasive, so *powerful,* that it was (still is) taken as the mode of translation of reality itself. Far from being real, however, it functioned as, and constructed, an *ideal,* as Stephen Heath suggests:

> *What must be more crucially emphasised is that the ideal of a steady position, of a unique embracing centre . . . is precisely that: a powerful ideal. To say this is not simply to acknowledge that the practice of painting from the Quattrocento on is far from a strict adherence to the perspective system but demonstrates a whole variety of accommodations (in certain paintings, for example,*

17

*buildings will be drawn with one centre according to central perspective while a separate centre will then be chosen for each human figure); it is also to suggest that there is a real utopianism at work, the construction of a code – in every sense a* vision *– projected onto a reality to be gained in all its hoped-for clarity much more than onto some naturally given reality.*[12]

It is an ideal of space, of position and, indeed, of vision itself. An *ideal;* for not only is perspective as a system false to the binocular nature of vision, not only is it false to the movement of the eye in constructing for it a fixed and static position, it is false also, as a system of representation inscribed on a two-dimensional surface, to the curvilinear nature of the sphere of vision. These realities are in a sense beside the point compared with the value of the ideal as such. More than that, though, they are actually necessary to the way in which it works. M.H. Pirenne has noted, for example, the contradiction between binocular vision and monocular perspective representation as follows:

*When we look binocularly at a flat picture, the visual angles involved are not quite the same for the two eyes, since the eyes are at different positions . . . if the objects depicted are supposed to be at different distances, their single picture in perspective will not present for the two eyes the characteristic disparities of visual angles which they would perceive in reality.*

*In binocular position the disparities between the array of angles corresponding to the eyes are different for the projection on a surface and for the actual objects. As stereoscopic vision indicates depth, or lack of depth, mainly on the basis of such disparities, it will as a rule show that the picture is only a surface.*[13]

Thus, when 'ordinary pictures are viewed in the usual manner, with both eyes, the spectator is aware of the characteristics of the picture surface, including its shape and position.'[14] Precisely. It is no accident that Pirenne himself goes on to note that this has its own advantages. It gives, he says, 'stability to the perception of the scene represented'.[15] It gives stability also to the ideal itself.

Like all visual representation, perspective is designed to engage and – mostly – to please the 'scopic drive', the desire to see, to gaze, to look. In order to do so, visual representations tend to organise and stabilise the elements they involve such that the look is both lured and contained. Perspective is one particular way of doing this. It is distinguished by the fact that look, eye and space are organised so as to match and reinforce one another, so as to achieve a smooth identity of object, on the one hand, and subject on the other.

12. Heath, 'Narrative Space', pp. 76–7

13. M.H. Pirenne, **Optics, Painting and Photography** (London: Cambridge University Press, 1970) pp. 77–8
14. Pirenne, **Optics, Painting and Photography**, p. 12
15. Pirenne, **Optics, Painting and Photography**, p. 12

Central to this organisation are the frame, and a notion of the surface of the picture as a window. The frame, like monocular perspective itself, is a phenomenon of the Renaissance:

> Before the fifteenth century, frames hardly exist, other than as the specific architectural setting that is to be decorated (wall, altarpiece, or whatever); it is during that century that frames begin to have an independent reality, this concomitant with the growth of the notion itself of a painting (the first instance of the use of the word 'frame' in an artistic sense recorded by the Oxford English Dictionary is c1600).[16]

The frame composes and organises the picture space and the scene it contains both for the look and the eye: 'The new frame is symmetrical (the centred rectangle, clearly "composable") and inevitable (the Quattrocento system cannot be realised without it, it becomes a reflex of "natural" composition)'.[17]

Just as the frame borders and packages an imaginary space, a depicted scene, so it also borders and packages a real space, the surface of the picture. An awareness of this surface is fundamental to painting. It is part of the pleasure it involves. But it is an awareness that oscillates and shifts. For the final component of monocular perspective as a system, a regime of vision, is that the surface should ideally function as a window, with the frame as the window's edge. Thus Alberti:

> Painters should know that they move on a plane surface with their lines and that, in filling the areas thus defined with colours, the only thing they seek to accomplish is that the forms of the things seen appear upon this plane as if it were made of transparent glass.'[18]

Or again, more emphatically:

> I describe a rectangle of whatever size I please, which I imagine to be an open window through which to view whatever is to be depicted there.'[19]

An apparent contradiction exists then between the notion of the surface as a window, as 'transparent glass', and the necessity for an awareness of surface as a surface. But it is only, indeed, apparent. It is a contradiction that is *managed*. For the window is the other side of the impossible ideal. The surface is necessary to register the marks of paint, thus to ensure, to return to Pirenne's remarks, that the scene, the image, does not move or shift; to ensure, in fact, that it is stable, that it constitutes a palpable identity. Only if this stability exists can monocular perspective construct its scenes so perfectly and centrally for the look of the individual eye.

---

16. Heath, 'Narrative Space', p. 81
17. Heath, 'Narrative Space', p. 81
18. Quoted in Panofsky, **Renaissance and Renascences in Western Art**, p. 120
19. Panofsky, **Renaissance and Renascences in Western Art**, p. 120

# Perspective and Photography

The camera obscura is the very instrument for the mechanical production of monocular perspective. Photography is the means by which it could mechanically and chemically be fixed, printed, marked and inscribed:

*Niepce, the successive adepts of the Daguerreotype, and those innumerable inventors who made photography what it is today were not actually concerned to create a new type of image or to determine novel modes of representation; they wanted, rather, to fix the images which 'spontaneously' formed on the ground of the camera obscura.*[20]

The camera obscura's image was fleeting, intangible, evanescent. It could only previously be registered by hand. As Fox Talbot's words indicate, the hand could be fallible. Silver compounds, however, could ensure perfection. Light, nature herself, drew the picture:

*No human hand has hitherto traced such lines as these drawings display; and what man may hereafter do, now that Dame Nature has become his drawing mistress, it is impossible to predict.*[21]

*the daguerreotype represents inanimate nature with a degree of perfection unattainable by the ordinary processes of drawing and painting — a perfection equal only to that of nature herself.*[22]

The aim of photography's inventors therefore, was

*to discover among the emanations of luminous liquid an agent which would be capable of imprinting in an accurate and durable way images transmitted by optical processes.*[23]

The 'optical processes' in question were those of monocular perspective, the 'natural images' produced were those of perspective representation, corrected, as Renaissance paintings had been, but corrected mechanically, automatically by the camera lens.[24] Moreover, where perspective painting was the product of an inscribed human labour, and where there was thus a mediation between the referent and its sign (hence a space for the mark of the artist), photography involved a bond, an existential link, between sign and referent, representation and reality. Furthermore, the image produced, as contemporaries were astonished to point out, far exceeded in detail the images produced by the artist. It was marked, indeed, by the *density* of reality itself. A view of Paris was described as 'drawing carried to a degree of perfection which Art can never attain. We count the paving stones; we see the humidity caused by the rain!'[25] As

20. Damisch, 'Five Notes for a Phenomenology of the Photographic Image', p. 71
21. Fox Talbot, quoted in Helmut and Alison Gernsheim, **The History of Photography**, pp 63–4
22. Joseph Louis Gay-Lussac, quoted in Gus Macdonald, **Camera**
23. Nicéphore Niepce, quoted in J-L Comolli, 'Technique and Ideology: Camera, Perspective, Depth of Field', in **Film Reader**, no. 2, p. 135
24. Monocular perspective involves and produces distortions as a consequence of the fact that the image is projected on to a vertical plane, producing a deviation in symmetry away from the centre of the picture and a consequent effect of curvature. Because the camera obscura produces monocular perspective exactly, it, too, produces these distortions, as can be witnessed by taking photographs with a pinhole camera. A lens is necessary to 'correct' these distortions, either in the camera obscura itself (as della Porta recommended), or else in the photographic camera proper. See Pirenne, **Optics, Painting and Photography**
25. Quoted in Aaron Scharf, **Art and Photography**, p. 28

26. Scharf, **Art and Photography**, p. 34
27. Eugene Delacroix, quoted in Scharf, **Art and Photography**, p. 119
28. Delacroix, quoted in Scharf, **Art and Photography**, p. 120
29. W.M. Ivins, **Art and Geometry** (New York: Dover, 1964), p. 108

Samuel Morse wrote, 'the exquisite minuteness of the delineation cannot be conceived. No painting or engraving ever approached it'.[26] What the technology of photography secured was, thus, perspective as reality, reality as perspective. The photograph was 'the mirror of the object',[27] it was 'literally true perspective'.[28]

*Strong as the mathematical convention of perspective had become in picture making before the pervasion of photography, that event definitely clamped it on our vision and our beliefs.*[29]

Photography was massively popular. Half a million photographic plates were being used in Paris in 1847. In Great Britain there were 51 people registered as professional photographers in 1851. Ten years later, that figure had risen to some 2879. There was a town on the Hudson river actually called Daguerreville, with a factory producing some three million daguerreotype plates per year. During the craze for *cartes-de-visite* (photographs mounted on visiting cards), it is claimed that Disdéri in Paris was taking £48,000 a year at an average of 200 sitters per day. The impact and spread of photography in all its forms was extraordinary.

The first daguerreotype camera, *c.* 1839. Made by Giroux. *Courtesy Kodak Museum*

30. The English engravers, Frederick Havell and James Tibbitts Willmore, quoted in Scharf, **Art and Photography**, p. 32

Niepce's heliograph and Daguerre's daguerreotype were processes that produced a positive print directly. Once the negative-positive process, initially developed by Talbot with his calotype, became established with wet-plate photography and the *carte-de-visite* in the 1850s, then the way was open for mass mechanical reproduction. The images drawn by the sun could thus 'be multiplied with perfect identity for ever!'[30]

Photography thus constituted an enormous social investment in perspective and its image of the world on the part of the industrialised countries. It therefore constituted also an enormous social investment in the centrality of the eye, in the category and identity of the individual, in a specific form of visual pleasure, and in an ideology of the *visibility* of the world. At the historical point at which industrialisation had on a massive scale restructured class conflict, threatened social identity and stability, transformed ideologies and processes of knowledge and riven great gaps in the social fabric, photography, with all the authenticity that science and the machine now had, re-inscribed perspective and its image of the world across these very gaps, differences and conflicts.

Strain, struggle and conflict were at their most intense in the urban centres. Hence the enormously powerful attraction of nature, both as a scene and a category, not only in the

Talbot's early calotype

photographs themselves, but also in the discourses around them. Nature was elsewhere, outside, other; it was grand, at times even terrifying, but its terror was not the fruit of human misery and conflict, of social upheaval and revolt. The domestic countryside and the countryside of the non-industrialised (colonised) lands provided a subject matter and a genre almost as popular as that of portraiture (which assured human dignity and identity in a different way):

*In none of these pictures do we see the least signs of man;*

not a log hut nor an axe-felled tree to indicate his presence: all seems wild, primitive nature, which gives great charm to these excellent photographs.[31]

The landscape photographer A.H. Wall in his book **Artistic Landscape Photography,** published in 1896, also saw the 'charm' of images of uninhabited nature, recommending the exclusion of all 'traces of human habitation, no sign of cottage or farm, cattle or cultivation'.[32] The complete eradication of all marks of human society, hence of all forms and traces of social being and social conflict. Contrast the urban centres, the towns and cities. But photography here, too, has its palliative role:

> Anyone who knows what the worth of family affection is among the lower classes, and who has seen the array of little portraits stuck over a labourer's fireplace, still gathering into one the 'Home' that life is always parting – the boy that has 'gone to Canada', the 'girl out at service', the little one with the golden hair that sleeps under the daisies, the old grandfather in the country – will feel with me that in counteracting the tendencies, social and industrial, which every day are sapping the healthier family affections, the sixpenny photograph is doing more for the poor than all the philanthropists in the world.[33]

> Photographic portraiture is the best feature of the fine arts for the million that the ingenuity of man has yet devised. It has in this sense swept away many of the illiberal distinctions of rank and wealth, so that the poor man who possesses but a few shillings can command a perfect lifelike portrait of his wife or child as Sir Thomas Lawrence painted for the most distinguished sovereigns of Europe.[34]

In thus 'democratising' perspective representation as object and possession, photography simultaneously 'democratised' the world as the sum total of its discrete individual images, society as the sum total of its discrete and individual points of view, and the eye and the look as that which unite all in a deeply troubled and convulsed society.

## Machines for the Production of Spectacle

Photography was by no means the only form of representation born in and around the nineteenth century to foster 'the idea of seeing for seeing's sake.[35] It was in fact only one of many instruments, institutions and practices designed to engage, aston-

---

31. **Illustrated London News** on the works of Californian photographers quoted in Alan Thomas, **The Expanding Eye** (London: Croom Helm, 1978) p. 34
32. Quoted in Thomas **The Expanding Eye,** p. 119
33. **Macmillan's Magazine,** 1871, quoted in Gus Macdonald, **Camera,** p. 5
34. **The Photographic News,** 1861, quoted in H. and A. Gernsheim, **The History of Photography,** p. 171
35. Sontag, **On Photography,** p. 93

ish and entertain the eye; only one of a vast array of machines for the production of spectacle. Together, they constitute a particular, historical regime of the gaze, a gaze whose mark photography in reflex fashion is actually able to catch:

*The features are admirably marked out and are perfectly correct whatever may be the size on which they are taken, as they are all reduced in proportion. The eyes appear beautifully marked and expressive, and the iris is delineated with a peculiar sharpness, as well as the white dot of light on it.*[36]

It is worth, initially, simply listing some of the arts and practices of spectacle that arose during the course of the latter half of the eighteenth century and during the course of the nineteenth century itself, in order to give some indication as to the size of the phenomenon in question. At random, then, they include the following: the Phantasmagoria, the Lampascope, the Diorama, the Panorama, the Betaniorama, the Europerama, the Cyclorama, the Cosmorama, the Giorama, the Pleorama, the Kalorama, the Kineorama, the Poccilorama, the Neorama, the Eidophusikon, the Nausorama, the Physiorma, the Typorama, the Udorama, the Uranorama, the Octorama, and the Diaphanorama. The features that united these instruments, arts and machines included on the one hand an 'astonishing' capacity for realism, for painstakingly detailed representation, and on the other a specific dependence on lighting effects; an extraordinary representational density coupled with a particular — usually mobile — regime of luminosity, such, precisely, as to lure, reflect and process the spectator's gaze.

36. **The Morning Chronicle,** 12 September 1840, quoted in H. & L. Gernsheim, **The History of Photography,** p. 92

Phantasmagoria

The Phantasmagoria, for example, consisted of slides projected from behind a translucent screen to an audience seated on the other side. Artificial lighting effects, the sights — and the sounds — of thunder and lightning accompanied what tended nearly always to be scenes suggestive of the supernatural. It is no accident that it was precisely during this period — and throughout the course of the nineteenth century — that there existed a whole theology of light as the trace of the noumenal in the real, as the mark of the spirit in matter:

> light . . . was the conduit between the world of sense impressions and the world of the spirit.[37]

> Beginning with Newton's view of light as corpuscular — made up of infinitely small particles — and adding to this the Cartesian notion that matter consists of particles that are indefinitely divisible, it was possible to think of light as a spectrum that begins in the world of the sense and shadows off into the world of spirits.[38]

Light as the very instance of the gap between the look, the image and the real.

The Eidophusikon, invented by the theatrical stage painter Philip de Loutherbourgh and opened in 1781, consisted of a small stage six feet wide by eight feet deep on which were shown model scenes, marked, again, by their ingenious lighting effects. In **A Storm at Sea** for instance:

> the clouds positively floated upon the atmosphere, and moved faster or slower, ascended or descended. Waves carved in soft wood and highly varnished undulated and threw up their foam, but as the storm began to rage, grew more and more violent, till at last their commotion appeared truly awful. The vessels, exquisite little models, rose and sank and appeared to move fast or slow according to their bulk and distance from the eye. Rain, hail, thunder and lightning descended in all their varying degrees of intensity and grandeur. Natural-looking light from the sun, the moon, or from artificial sources, was reflected naturally back wherever it fell upon a proper surface. Now the moonlight appeared sleeping on the wave, now a lurid flash lit up the tumultuous sea.[39]

Franz Niklaus König's Diaphanorama was first shown in Berne in Switzerland in 1815. König had been a successful landscape, genre and theatrical scene painter. The Diaphanorama consisted of water-colour paintings on a paper surface especially prepared to achieve a state of transparency. They were shown in a darkened room by transmitted and reflected light and consisted of 'romantic views of the moonlit Lake of Brienz, sunset

---

37. Rosalind Krauss, 'Tracing Nadar', **October** 5, p. 37
38. Krauss, 'Tracing Nadar', p. 39
39. A contemporary account quoted in Helmut and Alison Gernsheim, **L.J.M. Daguerre** (New York: Dover, 1968) p. 43

on the Jungfrau, and William Tell's Chapel by torchlight and moonlight'.[40] It proved so popular that it toured to other Swiss towns and then on to Germany and France, remaining in public exhibition until 1821.

The Panorama, developed initially by Robert Barker in 1787 and described by him as *'La Nature à coup d'ôeil'*, consisted of gigantic canvasses, especially lit, and often circling the spectators as they watched. As with the other devices mentioned, its feature was its painstaking detail and its display of spectacular lighting effects. As Dolf Sternberger has emphasised, the 'realism' was part of the display, appreciated simultaneously both for its verisimilitude and for its artifice. Referring to the German Panoramist, Anton von Werner, Sternberger writes as follows:

*In all the passages of his memoirs dealing with the panorama, Anton von Werner never once quotes the voice of naiveté, never once cites any evidence that visitors were really deceived — and this circumstance characterizes the painter's 'objective' aim and the expectation of contemporaries. Instead, Werner compiled a mass of testimonials by domestic and foreign colleagues, all of them very impressively confirming that this art of deception was done for its own sake and not . . . to deceive.*[41]

Later in the century the 'magic of both electricity and mechanical music . . . helped considerably to intensify the enchantment of the visitor and the quality of the panorama as mirage',[42] while in his **Evening at Sedan,** von Werner 'hit upon the idea of sculpturally modelling the lights — especially the weapons and musical instruments flashing in the sun — and then adding silver or gold', thus producing a 'scattered brilliance in a space otherwise filled with uniform studio light',[43] a shimmering of light and the look.

The Diorama, finally, provides a concrete and specific link with photography through the figure of Louis Daguerre, co-inventor of the Diorama, along with Charles-Marie Bouton, and inventor of the daguerreotype. The Diorama was described in its English patent specification as 'an improved Mode of publicly exhibiting Pictures or Painted Scenery of every Description and of distributing or directing the Day Light upon or through them, so as to produce many beautiful Effects of Light and Shade'.[44] Its popularity at its height was enormous (there were something like seventeen establishments showing Dioramas in one form or another in London alone), though it should be stressed that this popularity was specific. The Diorama, along with most of the other forms of scenic spectacle described here, was primarily addressed to, and attended and written about by, the bourgeoisie.

40. A. and H. Gernsheim, **L.J.M. Daguerre**, p. 14
41. Dolf Sternberger, 'Panorama of the 19th Century', **October** 4, pp 6–7
42. Sternberger, 'Panorama of the 19th Century', p. 9
43. Sternberger, 'Panorama of the 19th Century', p. 5
44. A. and H. Gernsheim, **L.J.M. Daguerre**, p. 14

Diorama

Alison and Helmut Gernsheim in their book on Daguerre describe the workings of the Diorama as follows:

*Like stage scenery, the pictures were set back from the auditorium . . . at the end of an enormous tunnel formed by screens . . . The spectator was seated in a dim light until the curtain was drawn up and the picture, lit up from the roof and from its rear, was revealed. Being painted on fine transparent linen, the effect was one of extraordinary beauty and reality of appearance. The great diversity of scenic effects was produced by a combination of translucent and opaque painting, and of transmitted and reflected light by contrivances such as screens and shutters.*[45]

Once again, then, the themes are verisimilitude and light, 'reality' and vision, nature and spectacle:

*The 'View of Brest Harbour' is not a vain representation — it is reality itself.*[46]

*The priests and the Levites take their place in the procession leading to the entrance; sacred music is heard, incense is burnt in honour of Jehovah, and from the midst of the clouds a miraculous light illuminates the Temple with its brilliance, dazzling the eyes of the people gathered in religious silence.*[47]

*This impression was strengthened by perceiving the light and shadows change, as if clouds were passing over the sun, the rays of which occasionally shone through the painted windows, casting coloured shadows on the floor . . . The illusion was rendered more perfect by the excellence of the painting, and by the sensitive condition of the eye in the darkness of the surrounding chamber.*[48]

We are clearly coming close at this point to some of the

45. A. and H. Gernsheim, **L.J.M. Daguerre**, p. 20
46. **The Mirror of Literature**, 2 October 1824, quoted in A. and H. Gernsheim, **L.J.M. Daguerre**, pp. 24–5
47. A review of 'The Inauguration of the Temple of Solomon', in the **Journal des Artistes**, 18 September 1836, quoted in A. and H. Gernsheim, **L.J.M. Daguerre**, p. 37
48. Frederick C. Bakewell, **Great Facts** (London, 1859), quoted in A. and H. Gernsheim, **L.J.M. Daguerre**, p. 16

basic effects and characteristics of the cinema — reality, vision, spectacle, movement. These effects and characteristics are not restricted to the Diorama. In combinations of twos and threes, so to speak, they are the constant themes not just of the Panorama and the Eidophusikon, not just of photography, not just of much nineteenth century painting (which deserves a whole chapter on its own). They can also be found in a whole series of mechanical toys and devices scattered across the nineteenth century history of the newly industrialised countries. Coinciding with — often the direct product of — massive research into the principles of optics and vision, and into new realms of the visible itself, coinciding also with the mechanised distribution of perspective across the totality of society, they prepare the way for the existence of cinema not only by embodying the principles that came to dominate cinema itself, but also by providing directly some of the technical conditions of its existence. In conjunction with developments in photography these toys and devices began in a very real sense to provide the cinema with its scientific, technical and ideological base.

# 2:

# Moving Pictures

## Optics and the Eye

The nineteenth century saw a marked resurgence of interest in science and technology in optics, vision and the eye. Thomas Young revived the wave theory of the propagation of light and published a paper on the action of the eye and on colour vision. Wollaston — inventor of the camera lucida — investigated the properties of the spectrum. Mathematical optics was revived with the rediscovery of projective geometry, the study of perspective by Gaspard Monge and others and the questioning of Euclidean principles. The properties of light were further studied by Fresnel, Arago and Maxwell. The invisible parts of the spectrum were studied by Herschel, de Saussure, Berard, Selbeck and others, while the first modern spectroscope was constructed by Meyerstein in 1856. Herman von Helmholtz published his monumental studies of the human eye and physiological optics in the 1850s and also invented the ophthalmoscope and the phakascope. In the related fields of scientific and optical technology, the nineteenth century also saw substantial developments in the field of lens construction, with improvements to the microscope and telescope and in the quality of optical glass (evidently of importance for both photography and film), the development of the first modern prism spectroscope and the use of silver rather than mercury as a backing for mirrors. All in all — and this is only the tip of the iceberg — a massive investment in exploring, exploiting and extending the properties of vision and the visible.

One of the major topics of optical research during the

nineteenth century was the phenomenon known as 'persistence of vision' or 'retention of the image'. The phenomenon itself is essential to cinema, since the impression of movement a film produces depends upon a series of static and separate images or frames being passed through the cine-projector at a particular speed. It is involved in cinema's prehistory inasmuch as a good deal of scientific research into 'persistence of vision' led directly to the production of a whole series of toys and amusements that exploited the effect in question and that constituted an important component in the regime of vision and spectacle that traversed the nineteenth century.

The nineteenth-century conception of 'persistence of vision' consisted basically in the notion that the retina in the eye retains an image of the impression it receives for a short but distinct period of time. According to this notion, the effect of movement produced by a film is explained as a consequence of this 'retention of the image': the human eye retains an impression of each of the frames on a strip of film long enough, as it were, for the next frame to be moved into place. A set of discrete images with a number of minimal differences in sequence, interspersed with a series of gaps, thus appears as one continual, moving image.

In Chapter Four of his book on early British cinema, **The Dream that Kicks,** Michael Chanan demonstrates that this particular conception of 'persistence of vision' is false, since it fails to account both for the role of the brain in perception and also, in fact, for the nature of the perception of movement itself. Chanan writes as follows:

*The trouble really begins with the notion of 'persistence of vision' itself. It is an unfortunate misnomer, especially when paraphrased as 'retention of the image'. There is, in fact, no retention at all, but* the inability of the eye to distinguish rapidly repeating stimuli beyond a certain threshold.[1]

Added to this particular effect, the threshold of perception itself, is another, that of the phenomenon of apparent movement. Both are involved together in the effects of perception produced and engaged by film. The phenomenon of apparent movement — the 'phi phenomenon' — is illustrated by an experiment in which two alternately flashing lights are placed next to one another: 'When the flashes alternate at a speed which goes beyond the threshold, the viewer no longer sees two lights flashing alternately, but a single light oscillating between two points.'[2]

Linking the two phenomena together Chanan finally

1. Michael Chanan, **The Dream that Kicks** (London: Routledge & Kegan Paul, 1980) p. 59
2. Chanan, **The Dream that Kicks,** p. 65

goes on to elaborate the concept of a 'perceptual threshold of duration': the minimum length of time a stimulus must last in order for it to be perceived, in Chanan's words, as *'lasting any time at all.'*[3] We see movement not because our eyes retain each image long enough for it to obliterate the following gap and dissolve into the next image, but because we do not see the gaps at all. They simply do not last long enough, they do not cross the perceptual threshold of duration.[4]

Accurate or not, nineteenth-century interest in persistence of vision produced a whole series of toys, amusements, instruments and machines which were designed both to exploit and to illustrate it. Various aspects of the phenomenon were studied by Young, Roget, Wheatstone, Horner, Faraday and Herschel in England, by Stampfer in Austria and by Plateau in Belgium. Faraday and Roget both wrote their studies on it in the early 1820s, and it was during this period too that one of the first of the scientific toys, the thaumatrope, was produced. Invented by Sir John Herschel and popularised by Dr D. A. Paris, the thaumatrope consisted simply of a disc with a drawing on both sides. When spun between the fingers, the two images merge into one. Paris manufactured the toy and wrote about it in his **Philosophy in Sport Made Science in Earnest** in 1827.

Two years later, in Belgium, Joseph Plateau wrote his influential doctoral thesis on the persistence of vision. A year after that, Faraday produced his Faraday's wheel, another early optical toy, and in 1833, Plateau produced his Phénakistiscope. The Phénakistiscope was one of the most important devices in the prehistory of cinema. It consisted of a disc with slots cut into it and a series of phase pictures drawn round the perimeter. When rotated in front of a mirror and viewed through the slots, the mirror image produces an effect of continuous motion. Plateau described the principle behind his device as follows:

*If a number of objects differing minimally in form and position are shown successively to the eye very rapidly and at sufficiently close intervals, the impressions they produce on the retina will coalesce without becoming confused, and you will believe you are looking at a single object changing gradually in form and position.*[5]

A very similar device, the Stroboscope, was invented in the same year in Austria by the geometrician Simon Ritter von Stampfer.

Other devices followed across the century in rapid succession: Horner's Zoëtrope, Dubosq's Bioscope or Stéréofantascope, Anschutz's Tachyscope, Reynaud's Praxinoscope,

3. M Chanan, **The Dream that Kicks**, p. 67
4. For an alternative description of the same phenomena see R. L. Gregory, **Eye and Brain** (London: Weidenfeld & Nicolson, 1966) pp. 109–111

5. Quoted in Georges Sadoul, **Histoire Générale du Cinéma**, vol. 1 (Paris: Editions Denoël, 1948) p. 17

Du Mont's Omniscope, Sellers' Kinematoscope, Beal's Choreutoscope, and Cook and Bonnelli's Photobioscope. All derived principally from the Phénakistiscope; all exploited and explored the principles of persistence of vision; and all fed directly and indirectly into establishing the conditions for the emergence of the cinema. It is no accident that the patent descriptions of at least two of these devices are resonant of the ideological themes that persistently accompany the cinema. Hence Jules Dubosq on his Stéréofantascope:

> With the mirror-stereoscope I finally succeeded in constructing a machine that could combine the essential properties of the Stereoscope with the marvellous qualities of M. Plateau's Fantascope or Phénakistiscope. The Stereoscope gives an impression of three-dimensionality while the Phénakistiscope provides an impression of movement. The Stéréofantascope or Bioscope, as its name indicates, achieves both effects simultaneously, the impression of relief and of movement, that is to say, the sensation of life itself.[6]

The sensation of life. Just add to this the phrase used by Henry Du Mont in his 1859 patent for the Omniscope, a device which like the Stéréofantascope was designed to produce moving images in relief. This device, in Du Mont's words, was simply 'for the pleasure of the eyes'.[7]

6. Quoted in **Le Cinéma des Origines, Cinéma d'Aujourd'hui** no. 9 (Autumn 1976) p. 35
7. Quoted in Jacques Deslandes, **Histoire Comparée du Cinéma** vol. 1 (Paris: Casterman, 1966–8) p. 80

## Rapid Photography: Muybridge and Marey

A number of these many devices, the Omniscope and the Stéréofantascope among them, involved the use of photographs. To that extent, they were dependent upon those techological developments in photography which permitted rapid, successive exposures. The very first photograph, one of Niepce's heliographs, had taken something like eight hours' exposure time. Exposure time for the daguerreotype and the calotype was several minutes — hence the absence of human figures in many of the early panoramic townscapes: the exposure time was so long that all that could be registered were stable and permanent objects.

Improvements were rapidly made. John Goddard discovered that by treating the silvered plate of the daguerreotype with bromine vapour its sensitivity could be greatly improved. Antoine Claudet showed that chlorine had a similar effect. Combined together, these two sensitising agents brought exposure times down to a few minutes and under. But this was still too slow to contemplate practically the use of photographs in apparatuses like the Phénakistiscope.

Ten years later, in 1851, Frederick Scott Archer introduced a new photographic process involving the use of collodion on a glass plate. Collodion was a newly discovered substance made by dissolving gun-cotton in ether. When used with potassium iodide to coat the glass plate, and when sensitised with silver nitrate, the resulting negative was found to be much more sensitive than either the calotype or the daguerreotype, and consequently exposure times were reduced again.

Muybridge's horse in motion

It was wet collodion plates that Eadweard Muybridge used in his famous experiments in recording photographically the movements of a race-horse. Muybridge was hired in the early 1870s by Leland Stanford to photograph one of his race-horses. After a period of little conclusive success, his researches were interrupted. Returning to them with improved apparatus he succeeded in taking some initial pictures in 1877, following them up a year later even more successfully by setting up a battery of cameras which were triggered by the horse as it moved through a

33

set of trip wires. Muybridge later went on to use gelatine-bromide dry plates (recently developed in England) during the course of a series of studies conducted at the University of Pennsylvania, later published under the title **Animal Locomotion.** He also adapted the zoëtrope for projecting the photographs he took. The photographs were arranged around the perimeter of a disc which was rotated by means of a handle. Light from the lamphouse of a conventional projection lantern was passed through each 'slide' as it stopped momentarily in front of a lens. The image produced was thrown by means of the light on to a large screen. Muybridge called his apparatus the zoogyroscope, later the zoopraxiscope. It was first used to project photographic images in motion to an audience at the San Francisco Art Association Rooms on 4 May 1880.

Zoopraxiscope

Muybridge later demonstrated his equipment and his work in Paris, and it was there that he met E. J. Marey, a physiologist who had also been working on the study and analysis of animal and human movement. In order to further his research Marey produced, in the winter of 1881–2, a device he called a photographic gun, an adaptation of the photographic revolver invented by Janssen in 1873 to study the transit of Venus across the sun. Working on roughly the same principle as the Colt automatic revolver, the mechanism within the photographic gun moved each photographic plate automatically in position once a previous shot had been taken, and enabled pictures to be taken at a very rapid rate. With financial aid from the French state and the city of Paris, Marey subsequently went on to develop a system

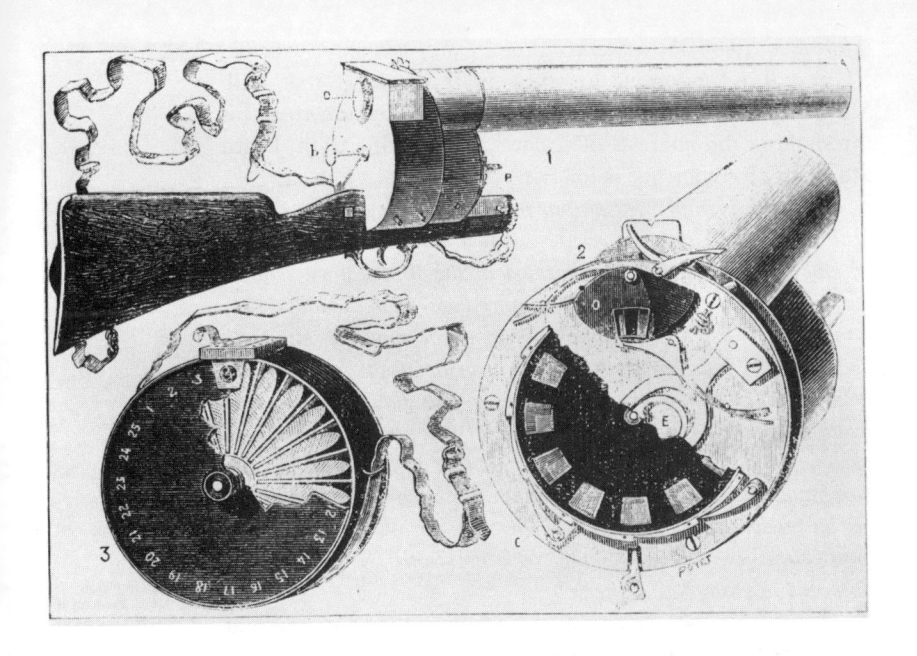

Marey's photographic gun

known as chronophotography, in which successive stages of movement were recorded on a single photographic plate.

Like Muybridge, Marey was dependent upon the enormous increase in the sensitivity of photographic plates brought about by the gelatin-bromide dry plate process and the consequent rapidity of exposure, a rapidity which, as Aaron Scharf has outlined, challenged fundamentally the authority of human vision and conventional visual representation alike, crossing the very threshold of visual appearance:

> With the appearance of more or less instantaneous photographs from about 1860, artists were faced with yet another and very fundamental problem. For many of these images defied the customary ways of depicting objects in motion and, though they were factually true, they were false as far as the human optical system was concerned. Was the artist then to confine his representations only to observable things, or was he justified in showing those which, as the instantaneous camera demonstrated, existed in reality yet could not be seen? Convention notwithstanding, it was now possible to learn to see many of the new and startling forms, or to perceive them on a threshold level, but the subjects of high speed photographs, taken from the 1870s, some with exposures as fast as 1/1000th and then, in the 1880s, 1/6000th of a second and less, could never be comprehended by the human eye alone. Though previously the photograph had been criticised for certain deficiencies of

*information, now the camera was accused of telling too much.*[8]

8. Aaron Scharf, **Art and Photography**, pp 14–15

It is important to stress in this context that both Muybridge and Marey were working precisely to cross this threshold in the interests of science and scientific truth, hence Muybridge's comments as follows:

*If it is impressed on our minds in infancy, that a certain arbitrary symbol indicates an existing fact; if this same association of emblem and reality is reiterated at the preparatory school, insisted upon at college, and pronounced correct at the university; symbol and fact — or supposed fact — become so intimately blended that it is extremely difficult to disassociate them, even when reason and personal observation teaches us they have no true relationship. So it is with the conventional galloping horse; we have become so accustomed to see it in art that it has imperceptibly dominated our understanding, and we think the representation to be unimpeachable, until we throw off all our preconceived impressions on one side, and seek the truth by independent observation from Nature herself.*[9]

9. Quoted in Aaron Scharf (ed), **Pioneers of Photography** (London: BBC, 1975) p. 128

Marey was even more insistent that research and analysis entailed not only breaking with age-old conventions of representation and perception but also breaking with the conventions of photography itself, the very ideology in which it was caught and which it hitherto had been used to support. He pushed it even further beyond the threshold of appearance by deconstructing its surface verisimilitude, its ability to produce a dense, detailed, homogenous image. In order to trace the shapes and pattern of movement, he did everything possible to break down the sensuous density of the photograph, posing his subjects in black against a carefully constructed black surface, with only white abstract shapes on various portions of the limbs to mark the stages of movement, replacing the seamless analogue of the conventional photographic image with posed, constructed and specifically arbitrary signs:

Marey's chronophotographic image formed with man walking when photographed against a black wall, c. 1884. *Courtesy Science Museum*

*Having established meticulously the pivotal points of the movements of the different joints, you stick on each of them a small shape of white paper: a circle here, a triangle there, a square, a cross, etc. When the animal is made to pass in front of the dark background, the photographic plate shows up an infinite number of little signs scattered in odd patterns. An enlargement of that image is projected on to a sheet of paper, and you note the repeats, because every fifth repetition of the given sign will stand out more clearly. Then you draw a line linking up the signs of the same image and you obtain a figure . . . which charts the different positions of the limbs and of the body . . .*[10]

Although Marey, like Muybridge, experimented with projecting the images he took, thus reconstituting the smooth movement that the images themselves deconstructed for analysis, he was not interested at all in the projection and the reconstitution of movement for its own sake. His experiments revealed the fallibility of the human eye. His apparatus was designed not to feed and exploit that fallibility, restoring to the eye an authority it could not of its own possess, but both to reveal and to correct it, thus enabling the proper study of visual phenomena. In the preface to a book written in 1899, he stressed this point in reference to photographs of movement:

*But in the end, what [the images] show could have been perceived with the naked eye. They add nothing to the power of our sight, they in no way diminish our illusions. Whereas the true nature of scientific method is to remedy the insufficiency of our senses and to correct their errors. In order to achieve this, chronophotography must stop trying to reproduce the phenomena as we see them.*[11]

Janssen, the inventor of the photographic revolver, simply summed up the difference between his apparatus and that of the phénakistiscope as follows:

*Compared with the phénakistiscope, it could be said that the photographic revolver solves the opposite problem. M. Plateau's phénakistiscope is designed to reproduce the illusion of movement by means of the series of elements that comprise the movement. The photographic revolver, on the other hand, provides the analysis of a phenomenon by reproducing the series of its basic component elements.*[12]

Photography initially confirmed the power of the human eye, setting it in place as the very point of coherence and significance, as, indeed, the very point of view. As the rapidity of exposure times increased, an optimum point was reached: the real was seized in all its evanescent detail, held in suspension at a point

[10] Quoted in Deslandes, **Histoire Comparée du Cinéma**, p. 127

[11] Quoted in Sadoul, **Histoire Générale du Cinéma**, p. 89
[12] Quoted in Sadoul, **Histoire Générale du Cinéma**, p. 66

where the eye was still comfortable, still entertained by the glossy aura of exactitude, an aura summed up between the lines, so to speak, of the following review of some of Charles Breeze's instantaneous studies of the sky and the sea:

> Every drop of water in the waves dashing and breaking against the rock and tumbling headlong into the foaming cataract; the seagulls skimming across the wave, the ocean lashed into turbulence by the tempest, rare sunset and moonlit views, are amongst his triumphs.[13]

But there was a point at which the comfort and the aura were shattered, to reveal strange, disconcerting shapes, the realms outside normal human vision, the unknown. In that shock to pleasure, certainty, easy identification, was the psychological possibility of death, the major theme of the late nineteenth century. It is no accident that death was therefore the major theme that accompanied reviews and reports of these experiments beyond the realms of appearance and the devices that turned them back to the realms of familiarity — the phénakistiscope, the stroboscope, the praxinoscope and the rest. In restoring motion to the fragmented images, they restored them, almost literally, back to life, thus ensuring simultaneously the return of the authority of vision, the return of the aura of reality, and the return of the rhythms of pleasure. Muybridge's experiments in projection, and the reports that accompanied them, are a good indication. The first, a report in **Le Temps** dated 29 November 1881, links moving photographs to the general achievements of science in the nineteenth century in warding off the threat of death:

> Imagine: with the telephone [read 'phonograph'] you can already preserve the human voice in a box, just like sweets; with a series of animated photographs you will be able, years later, to rediscover the way a man moves or holds his head. The ghost will walk, and that is how little by little science, progressing with giant steps, will succeed in abolishing death, its sole obstacle and only enemy.[14]

The second, a recollection by C.H. Bothamley of a demonstration given by Muybridge at a Yorkshire college, hints symptomatically at the very pleasure and fascination upon which cinema, in its various forms, depends. Aura, beauty, motion, vision and light cross another in a rhythm of repetition which provides the very mark of pleasure itself. Bothamley writes as follows:

> The plates carrying the successive images were fixed to a large glass disk, which rotated between the condenser and the lens, while an opaque disk with transparent slits in it rotated in the

13. Quoted in A. and H. Gernsheim, **L.J.M. Daguerre**, p. 201

14. Quoted in Deslandes, **Histoire Comparée du Cinéma**, p. 101

opposite direction. *The results surprised as much as they delighted the large and somewhat critical audience before which they were shown. Perhaps the most striking of all the demonstrations was that of the wing motion of a large white bird (a cockatoo, I believe). As the wings moved in the upstroke, brilliantly lighted by the sunshine, we saw most distinctly every plume of the wing turn on its base, so as to present only its edge in the direction of motion, and thus offer as little resistance to the air as possible. As the wing came down, each plume turned back so as to present its flat surface to the air and thus gain the maximum impulse. I well remember the murmur of astonishment and pleasure that went through the whole audience, and the persistent demands for the repetition of what was as beautiful a picture as I have ever seen on a screen.*[15]

15. C.H. Bothamley. 'Early Stages of Kinematography' in Raymond Fielding (ed), **A Technological History of Motion Pictures and Television** (Berkeley: University of California Press, 1967) p. 7

By the late 1880s, the technical conditions for the existence of the cinema existed. High-speed photography and camera apparatuses with the capacity to take a series of rapidly successive photographs had been developed. Machines adapted from Plateau's Phénakistiscope now had the capacity to project photographic images at a rate sufficient to produce the illusion of motion. As well as those machines which fed directly into the development of the cinema, there existed a plethora of devices for the entertainment of the eye. Apart from those already mentioned above, there were numerous adaptations of the magic

A mid-Victorian magic lantern show. *Courtesy Bernard Howarth-Loomes*

lantern, ranging from Child's Dissolving Views through to the enormously complex Leviathan of the 1890s, each used to tell stories by means of painted or photographic slides and each

lantern, ranging from Child's Dissolving Views through to the enormously complex Leviathan of the 1890s, each used to tell stories by means of painted or photographic slides and each simulating movement by means of rapidity of projection and complex lighting arrangements. Reynaud's Praxinoscope had developed into the Théâtre Optique. Le Roy's Zoogyroscope had been produced in 1875, Rudge's Bio-Fantascope in 1880, and Anchütz' Phototachyscope in 1891. Numerous designs for what were in effect cine-cameras had been produced by Louis Le Prince, Donisthorpe and Croft, Albert Londe and others.

All these machines, apparatuses and devices became part and parcel of the specific regime of vision and spectacle that dominated the industrialised societies of the nineteenth century. What the apparatuses of animated photography achieved was an annulment — a containment — of the threats posed by photography elsewhere, the threats of discomfort, deconstruction, and death. When the cinema arrived it inscribed indelibly — in its technology as much as in its films — the hegemony of vision, spectacle, reality, life and movement across the complex and contradictory societies of the late nineteenth century.

# 3:

## The Invention of the Cinema

### Camera, Film and Projector

By 1895, the technological apparatus basic to the existence of the cinema — camera, film and projector — had been invented and developed almost simultaneously in the foremost industrialised countries of the world, the United States, Great Britain, Germany and France. On 28 December that year, the Lumières' Cinématographe projected its first films before a paying audience at the Grand Café on the Boulevard des Capucines in Paris. Technology, aesthetics, ideology and economics here come together in the first public appearance of an apparatus producing and circulating a new and specific form of signification, representation and entertainment.

Most of the machines developed in these countries — the Cinématographe in France, the Bioscope in Germany, the Animatograph in Britain, the Vitascope in America — were in one way or another derived, inspired or affiliated to either the Kinetograph, a moving picture camera, or the Kinetoscope, a peep-show viewing machine, both of which had been invented by W.K.L. Dickson at Thomas Edison's research laboratory at West Orange in America. According to Edison's own account, these inventions were motivated initially by a wish to produce recorded moving images to accompany the recorded sounds of his newly-invented phonograph:

*When I first turned my mind to the subject in 1887, it was with the thought of creating a new art. I was not interested in analysing motion because that had been done with brilliant success*

Edison's kinetoscope

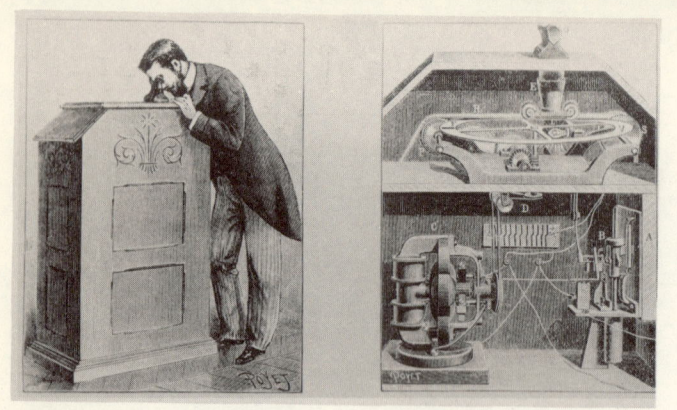

*by Muybridge and Marey before me. Just as with the phonograph, which makes a permanent record of an indefinite number of sounds, I wanted to make a permanent record of an indefinite number of successive phases of movement, doing for the eye what the phonograph had done for the ear.*[1]

As Edison's remarks imply, both he and Dickson knew of the various apparatuses devised by Muybridge and Marey, and the invention both of the Kinetograph and the Kinetoscope were influenced by the principles they embodied. The Kinetograph, for which a number of patents were issued as it evolved, was a large, heavy and somewhat cumbersome machine. It was used initially to take microphotographs for arrangement on a cylinder illuminated by a Geister spiral tube — the cylinder echoing the principles of the phonograph. Subsequently, however, it was used to take standardised strips of photographs, impelled intermittently in the camera by a clock escapement movement. At this point, the Kinetograph used a 1½ inch focus lens to produce pictures that were ¼ inch square, though both the lens capacity and the size of the photographs were soon enlarged.

The Kinetoscope was first constructed in 1890, and a patent for it issued in March 1893. Gordon Hendricks, in his book on the Kinetscope, gives the dimensions of the Kinetoscope as 18 inches by 27 inches by 48½ inches and goes on to quote Herman Casler's description of the machine as given in a lecture in 1909 in New York:

*A ribbon of transparent film carrying the pictures is laced up and down over idle spools at the lower part of the case. The ends of the film are joined, forming an endless band passing over two guide drums near the top of the case. One of these drums is driven by motor and feeds the film along by means of sprocket teeth which*

1. Quoted in F.H. Richardson, 'What Happened in the Beginning', in Raymond Fielding (ed), **A Technological History of Motion Pictures and Television** (Berkeley: University of California Press, 1967) p. 23

*engage with perforations along the edges of the film. Just above the film is a shutter wheel having five spokes and a very large rectangular opening in the rim directly over the film. An incandescent lamp . . . is placed below the film between the two guide drums, and the light passes up through the film, shutter opening, and magnifying lens . . . to the eye of the observer placed at the opening in the top of the case.*

*The film had a continuous motion, and, I believe showed pictures at the rate of forty per second. The shutter was probably about 10" in diameter and, judging from the photograph, the opening must be about ³⁄₄" wide. As the shutter made one revolution for each picture, the length of exposure would be between 1/1600 and 1/1700 part of one second.*[2]

2. Quoted in Gordon Hendricks, **The Kinetoscope** (New York: Beginnings of the American Film, 1966) p. 14

As Casler's description illustrates, and as Dickson's and Edison's accounts also stress, a feature essential to both the Kinetograph and the Kinetoscope was the film itself. Its basic properties were firstly the fact that it was made of celluloid, and was therefore both strong and flexible, and secondly that it was perforated, thus allowing it to be drawn evenly through the mechanisms of the Kinetograph and the Kinetoscope by a sprocket. Just as the intermittent motion of the Kinetograph was derived and adapted from the escapement mechanism of a watch, so the perforations in the film were derived and adapted from the perforations in the paper of the automatic telegraph (which Edison had also invented). The celluloid film that Dickson and Edison used was provided by George Eastman. Celluloid, a derivative of cellulose, was invented in 1861 by Alexander Parkes and was used as a substitute for ivory in the manufacture of billiard balls, false teeth, tubes, valves, taps and pistons. John Carbutt, an English photographer who had emigrated to America, first introduced emulsion-coated celluloid film into photography as an alternative to glass plates. It was Carbutt who first supplied Edison and Dickson with celluloid for their film, though in original form it existed as thin sheets, not as strips. Once roll-film had begun to be produced, however, it was Eastman who had captured the market. It was Eastman with whom a deal for the regular provision of celluloid roll film was eventually made once the Kinetoscope, and the films made for it, were being commercially produced and exploited.

A syndicate headed by A. O. Tate, Thomas Lombard and Erastus Benson first saw the commercial potential of the Kinetoscope and so acquired a concession from Edison to market it. The world's first Kinetoscope parlour opened on 14 April 1894 at 1155 Broadway in New York City. It proved so popular and profitable that within a year the syndicate, which now included three new partners, Norman Raff, Frank Gammon, and Andrew Holland, had installed Kinetoscopes in stores, hotels and parlours in cities throughout the country. Meanwhile another firm, headed by Frank Maguire and Joseph Baucus, acquired the foreign rights and began to market the Kinetoscope abroad.

A Broadway kinetoscope

The Lumière Cinématographe, 1896. *Courtesy Kodak Museum*

It was while the Kinetoscope was in Paris that it was first seen by the Lumière brothers, Auguste and Louis, and it was upon seeing it and thinking about the possibilities of projecting the films on to a screen for an audience that they began in 1894 to work on their own apparatus, the Cinématographe. The Cinématographe differed from Edison's machines first in that it combined two distinct functions, filming and projection, secondly in that it shot and projected film at a much lower (and therefore more economical) rate (16 frames per second as opposed to around 40 frames per second), thirdly in that it was relatively light and portable (weighing 5 kilos in comparison with the 500 kilos of the Kinetograph), and fourthly in that its projecting mechanism, like its filming mechanism, included an intermittent device, which consisted of a sliding block driven with a vertical motion by means of a triangular eccentric. The block stopped completely at the top and bottom of its motion thus enabling the film to keep stationary exactly on the axis of the lens of the machine. The Lumières at first used paper roll film, but later obtained celluloid base film from America and coated it with sensitive emulsion themselves.

The Lumières first demonstrated their machine to the Société d'Encouragement pour l'Industrie Nationale in Paris on 18 March 1895. The first film shown was a film of workers leaving their factory in Lyons. Both facts are resonant of the social and historical context and significance of the invention of the cinema and of the mode and relations of production of the technology it involved.

The Lumières were wealthy and successful businessmen. With their father Antoine they had in 1893 founded the first

**La Sortie des usines Lumière à Lyon** (Louis Lumière, 1895)

factory in Europe to produce photographic products and accessories. On an initial capital sum of 3 million francs they were, by the following year, producing 15 million photographic plates and employing some 300 workers. They thus had both the capital and the scientific and technical expertise with which to produce a machine related to the work in which they were already commercially involved. Indeed, as Peter Wollen has argued, they regarded the invention of the Cinématographe as a simple task in comparison with their work on colour photography.[3]

The immediate institutional context for the emergence of the Kinetograph and the Kinetoscope is just as significant. With the profits made from the invention of the telegraph, Edison had invested in a research laboratory to explore and exploit the commercial potential of electricity. He employed a team of scientists and technicians, of whom Dickson was one, precisely to

3. Peter Wollen, 'Cinema and Technology: A Historical Overview', in Teresa de Lauretis and Stephen Heath (eds), **The Cinematic Apparatus** (London: Macmillan, 1980) p. 15

Le Goûter du bébé (Louis Lumière, 1895)

invent new machines and new technological devices, his practice being to apply for patents on all possible developments in order to gain a monopoly — and hence access to any profits — on the products that his team might produce. His laboratories were a first step in the direction of the corporate-owned research laboratory, and through his companies, Edison General Electric, later General Electric, he had access to enormous funds.

## Technology and Commerce, Cinema and Profit

The cinematographic apparatus, then, was evolved and produced in the specific context of profitable capitalist industrial enterprises. And of course, its more general context was particularly that of capitalism and industry, since the conditions of existence of its technological base included specific developments in precision engineering, chemistry and chemical technology (especially in the case of celluloid), and mass production and industrial standardisation.[4] Moreover, that context in turn shaped the subsequent growth and development of the industry, the apparatus and its technology. Receipts from the first year on Edison's Kinetoscope in New York were something like 16,000 dollars; between 1894 and 1897 the Kinetoscope made over 48,000 dollars. For reasons of profitability alone, Edison was initially opposed to developing a projector, despite the pleas of his agents.

The Lumières, meanwhile, were making up to 7000 francs a week, and in January 1896 they invested some 300,000 francs in a film production company. As has been noted above, and as Vincent Pinel has pointed out, even the speed at which they shot and projected their films, a speed that was rapidly to become the standard, was 'a satisfactory compromise between two contradictory necessities, the one technological (there must be as many images as possible to reduce scintillation), the other commercial (there must be as few images as possible in order to diminish the cost . . .)'.[5] As Roy Armes has put it: 'Louis Lumière's contribution to the engineering side of the cinema is quite small — he merely devised a way of synchronising the shutter movement of the camera with the movement of the strip of photographic film — and if he had done no more than this, he would merit little more than a footnote in the books of film history. His real importance lies elsewhere . . . he established the cinema as an industry'.[6] Armes' sentiments with respect to Louis Lumière are echoed by Deslandes with respect to Edison:

*The essential act, the point of departure which finally led to the practical realization of animated projections, was the nickel which the American viewer dropped into the slot of the Edison kinetoscope, the 25 centimes which the Parisian stroller paid in*

---

[4]. See, in particular, Chanan, **The Dream that Kicks** and Jeanne Allen, 'The Industrial Context of Film Technology: Standardisation and Patents', in de Lauretis and Heath, **The Cinematic Apparatus**

[5]. Vincent Pinel, **Louis Lumière** (Paris: Anthologie du Cinéma no 78, 1974) p. 408
[6]. Roy Armes, **Film and Reality** (Harmondsworth: Penguin 1974) pp. 22–3

September 1894 to glue his eyes to the viewer of the kinetoscope . . .

This is what explains the birth of the cinema show in France, in England, in Germany, in the United States . . . Moving pictures were no longer just a laboratory experiment, a scientific curiosity; from now on they could be considered a commercially viable public spectacle.[7]

The cinematic apparatus developed in the context of specific historical, industrial and commercial conditions. Its technology continued to be refined because it was profitable — hence the rash of adaptations and improvements that followed the initial appearance — and success — of the Edison and Lumière machines. The most important of these included: Thomas Armat's Vitascope, a projector using a loop-forming mechanism (enabling the film to be drawn through the projector without being strained by the pulling and jerking involved in the workings of the intermittent device) and an intermittent movement which reduced flicker by giving the pictures a lengthy period of rest in front of the lamp; Armat's star-wheel intermittent device, by which a small sprocket carrying the film could be given a gradually accelerated intermittent movement without wearing the film or jarring the mechanism; Albert Smith's framing device, which enabled the frame projected on to the screen to be perfectly matched to the frame provided by the screen itself; and John Pross's shutter, which reduced scintillation and flicker.

What is important about all these innovations in this context is first that they all concern the projector (and hence exhibition) and secondly that most, if not all, form the basis for subsequent patent disputes. As Peter Wollen has noted, the commercial, industrial and economic pressures involved in mainstream film-making have often exerted themselves most fully at the point of exhibition.[8] Meanwhile, the role of patents in the establishment and evolution of the industry is absolutely crucial. The history of patent laws is given in outline in Michael Chanan's book, **The Dream that Kicks**.[9] What is important about the functioning of these laws in the late nineteenth century is that they began to form the basis of corporate control of sectors of the market:

*As a principal foundation of commercial success, patents in the second half of the nineteenth century increasingly became less the domain of a single inventor and entrepreneur who founded a manufacturing business and more a product of research departments — factories of invention — of major electrical and chemical industries. Gradually patent law, designed to protect the inventor's*

7. Jacques Deslandes, **Histoire Comparée du Cinéma** (Paris: Casterman, 1966) pp. 213–4

8. Wollen, 'Cinema and Technology', p. 19
9. Chanan, **The Dream that Kicks**, pp. 85–6

*right to the commercial benefits of invention, became industry's loophole to acquire the fruits of monopoly by buying patent rights, hiring inventors, and developing branches of engineering research to maintain superiority in patent production and control.*[10]

As far as the cinema is concerned, the commercial importance of patents on technology and equipment is stressed quite bluntly in Michael Conant's account:

*The motion picture industry was founded on a grant of monopoly in the form of the patent issued to Edison on his motion picture camera, invented in 1889. The camera was followed shortly by Edison's Kinetoscope cabinet viewer or 'peep-show', which was patented in 1891 . . . A rival firm, the Biograph company, was founded soon after. It had patented a camera designed to circumvent Edison's patents and used a larger film than the Edison camera. It also had patents on another type of cabinet viewer, the mutoscope.*[11]

The early years of cinema in the United States is littered with patent disputes, since Edison sued as many individuals and enterprises as he could in order to protect his monopoly and his profits, until in 1908, a combine, the Motion Picture Patents Company, was formed from the major patent-holding companies precisely to achieve full monopoly control over the market in film in America. The importance of patents and patent legislation in the articulation of the economy and technology is further evident where patents were absent. Edison did not take out a patent on his Kinetograph and Kinetoscope in Europe. It was precisely for this reason that Robert Paul entered the film business in England. He started by making duplicates of the Kinetoscope, moving into the production of films when Edison refused to supply his machine with the films he had produced for it.

The cinematic apparatus was evolved and produced in the specific context of profitable capitalist industrial enterprises. The conjunction of a series of separate technological and scientific developments — in optics, chemistry, engineering, mechanics — it emerged from specific economic conditions — and produced spectacular economic results. But the cinematic apparatus is more than a set of machines, is not just a technology. It is also, as Metz has put it 'a mental machinery'.[12]

If cinema was a conjunction of disparate developments, it was, and by and large still remains, a conjunction homogenised by a set of specific terms that emerge with constant, repetitive insistence across reviews, articles and theses that proliferate around the early films and around the first appearances of the apparatus itself: vision, life, reality, movement — and death.

10. Jeanne Allen, 'Copyright Protection in the Theatre, Vaudeville and Early Cinema', **Screen**, vol. 21, no. 2, Summer 1980

11. Michael Conant, **Antitrust in the Motion Picture Industry** (Berkeley: University of California Press, 1960) pp. 16–17

12. Metz, 'The Imaginary Signifier', p. 19

# Life, Death and Movement

An advertisement for Edison's Kinetoscope published in the **Washington Evening Star** on 8 October 1894 reads as follows:

It is here! Edison's Kinetoscope!!! Marvellous! Realistic! True to Life! The Most Wonderful and Interesting Invention of This Century of Science. The only actual and literal 'Living Pictures' ever produced.[13]

Allowing for the hyperbole (itself an important feature of the discourses around this new apparatus); allowing too for the particular stress on the role of science (again important, and a point to which I shall return), the terms used in this advertisement are very much the terms that recur across all the writings, not only on the Kinetoscope, but also on the Cinematographe and subsequent cinematic devices. 'Actual', 'literal', 'Realistic', 'True to Life'. The cinema is an illusion of the real. But more, it is a spectacle of movement. And as such it seems at times to exceed reality itself. To be more real than the real. At any rate, it is life itself, possessing, indeed, the power to undo the work of the death that it also, curiously but insistenly, entails.

13. Quoted in Hendricks, **The Kinetoscope**, p. 63

The illusion is complete and the effect marvellous.

The images come to life before your eyes and move, walk and dance as if they were flesh and bone.

It is, in effect, a Lilliput world — but with real life, because there seems to be a soul in the body of the little figures.[14]

These terms occur uniformly in descriptions both of the Kinetoscope and of the Cinématographe, but if anything, the latter is more realistic, more life-like, more astonishing, more spectacular, despite the fact that the subject matter of the films for the Kinetoscope was in itself more conventionally spectacular than the subject matter of the Lumières' films. Dickson shot his films either in or around his purpose-built studio — the Black Maria — and he tended to film theatrical acts or scenes, as the titles of the films themselves illustrate: **Shoeshine and the Barber Shop, Madame Bertoldi, Contortionist, The Gaiety Girls, Colonel Cody's Shooting Skill, Colonel Cody and his Sioux Indians, Sandow in Feats of Strength, Mexican Knife Thrower, Japanese Dancers, Milk White Flag** (a play) and **Police Raid on a Chinese Opium Den.** The scenes and figures themselves were smaller than those seen by the spectators of the Cinématographe, simply by virtue of the fact that they were viewed in a peep-hole machine rather than thrown life-size on to a screen. This difference was certainly one that was commented on. But in a sense more important was the contrast between the theatricality (and artifice)

14. A description of the Kinetoscope in the Mexican Paper **El Monitor Republica**, quoted in Hendricks, **The Kinetoscope**, p. 66

Shoeshine and the Barber Shop (W.K.L. Dickson, 1894)

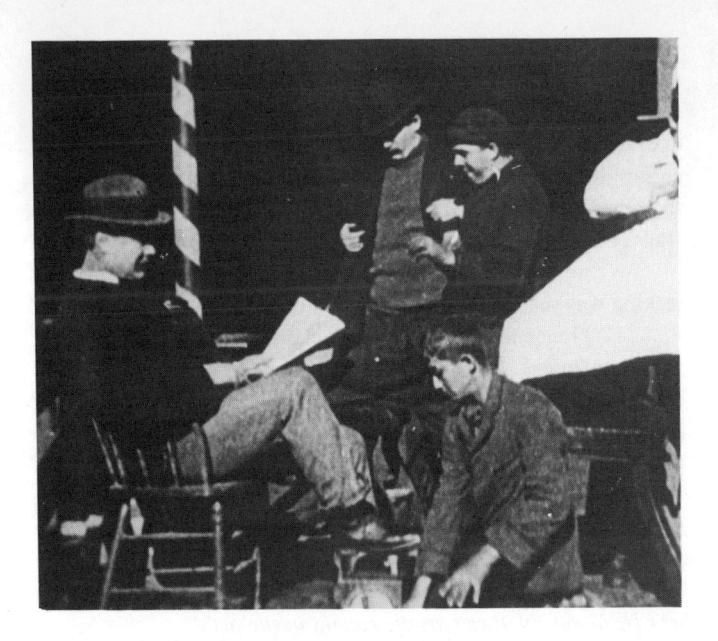

of the Kinetoscope films, and the presence of nature and the open-air in the Lumières' films:

> Another reason for the Cinématograph's fascination stems from the complexity of its images. Optical games relying on direct observation, chronophotography and the kinetoscope all required their images to be simple, almost schematic if they were to be legible. For instance, in the kinetoscope, the decor was reduced to a few simple elements or even to its most basic form: a black background. In addition, the eyepiece gave a small, flat image of the scene. 'It was lilliputian and seen as if through the wrong end of a telescope', a journalist noted.[15]

15. Pincl, **Louis Lumière**, p. 414

Scale, nature, depth. All these were indeed provided by the Cinématographe, alongside those qualities embodied in the Kinetoscope, though here the latter were amplified to an astonishing and abundant degree:

> The kinetoscope was able to render a good image of a scene, but it was very small and only one person could look at it. With the Cinématograph, many people can watch at the same time because it projects the image onto a screen, and each tableau lasts at least a minute. The human figures are large and scenes have a greater sense of depth because it succeeds in representing movements in streets, public places, etc. By the very fact that objects approximate their natural size, the illusion is heightened and becomes startingly real.[16]

16. Georges Sadoul, **Louis Lumière** (Paris: Cinèma d'Aujourd'hui, Editions Seghers, 1964) p. 34

Nothing could illustrate more forcefully the importance of the invention of the projector and projection. Photographs and drawings had been projected for years by the magic lantern operators, sometimes, indeed, with effects of movement and continuity provided by the technique of dissolving one slide into the next. But, like the realistic scenery on the nineteenth-century stage, what was lacking in the magic lantern shows was the detail of movement. More than that, and more precisely, what was lacking was the wind, the very index of real, natural movement.

Hence the obsessive contemporary fascination, not just with movement, not just with scale, but also with waves and sea-spray, with smoke and steam, with the effervescence of motion that the wind — and the cinema — alone seemed able to provide:

*You could see the iron begin to glow in the fire, becoming longer and longer under the blows of the hammer and, when plunged into the water, give off a cloud of steam, slowly rising in the air and then suddenly dispersed by a gust of wind. In Fontanelle's words, it was 'Nature herself, caught in the act'.*[17]

*Animated photographs are little marvels. All the details can be distinguished: the whirls of smoke curling upwards, waves breaking onto the beach, the flutter of leaves in the wind.*[18]

This kind of movement was the ultimate guarantee of the real:

*The spectator's fascination, breathlessly attempting to register every detail, has manifestly been excited by the overwhelming multiplicity of detail which, in itself alone, renders any sort of trickery or optical subterfuge impossible.*[19]

This movement — at last — enabled cinema to definitively surpass those other cultural apparatuses of vision and spectacle, photography and the theatre:

*Photography has stopped pinning down immobility. It perpetuates the image of movement.*[20]

*That settles scenery. Painted trees that do not move, waves that get up a few feet and stay there, everything in scenery we simulate on our stages will have to go. When art can make us believe that we see actual living nature, the dead things of the stage must go.*[21]

If motion — 'natural' motion, the *spectacle* of natural motion, in all its varied detail — was what marked the Cinématographe in particular, it was a specific kind of motion based on a specific use of the properties of the camera. And if it was motion

17. André Gay, quoted in Jean Mitry, **Histoire Générale du Cinéma**, vol. 1 (Paris: Editions Universitaires, 1969) p. 75

18. Henri de Parville, quoted in Sadoul, **Louis Lumière**, p. 30

19. **Le Moniteur de la Photographie,** April 1895, quoted in Pinel, **Louis Lumière**, p. 414

20. **La Poste,** 30 December 1895, quoted in Sadoul, **Louis Lumière**, p. 119

21. The theatrical producer Charles Frohman, quoted by A.R. Fulton in 'The Machine', in Tino Balio (ed.) **The American Film Industry** (Madison: The University of Wisconsin Press, 1976) p. 31

that created an overwhelming sense of life, it was motion that embodied, simultaneously, a threat of death. It was this threat, above all, that the conventions of cinematic representation that were developed over the years functioned to contain.

The cinema was based — its success and fascination were founded — upon the synthesis (rather than the analysis) of movement. Its technology was capable of either. But it came overwhelmingly to be used to produce the former rather than the latter. And it was this fact that damned it as useless in the eyes of many contemporary scientists. Albert Londe's piece in **Le Chasseur Français** (May 1896) remains in this respect the classic statement:

> The brothers Lumière, putting to use and connecting the ideas of their precursors, have produced an apparatus about which a great deal of fuss has been made. It is based on the principle of stopping the film, an idea that indisputably belongs to Marey, and it uses rolls of a certain length, something Edison had done before. It doesn't contain any new ideas whatsoever and its success as a curiosity with the public was due to their eagerness to see experiments that hadn't yet emerged from the laboratories, and above all to the clever publicity campaign conducted by capitalists with an interest in the success of a matter which is, more than anything else, financial.
>
> The reader may wonder why nobody has preceded the Lumières on this road. Two reasons may explain this. Firstly, from a scientific point of view, the photographic analysis of movement is far more important . . . The second reason is a question of money. Making synthesis available through photography is an extremely expensive business, because it involves using up reels of very costly film in a few seconds, and frankly speaking, ordinary individuals or even state laboratories cannot embark on such an expensive project while yielding so little in terms of real progress.
>
> Only American-type initiatives, such as the one at Parc d'Orange where Edison places his inventions at the disposal of companies charged with their exploitation, or associations of capitalists, were in a position to derive benefits from principles that were known but not yet applied for the reasons indicated earlier.[22]

Movement is simultaneously for the perpetuation of human vision and the human eye and for the generation of money and profit. The former through the latter. Hence Edison marks the difference between analytic cinematography and his own practice precisely as a difference in the position and function of the eye:

> I wanted to make a permanent record of an indefinite

22. Quoted in Deslandes, **Histoire Comparée du Cinéma**, pp. 232–3

*number of successive phases of movement, doing for the eye what the phonograph had done for the ear. This meant the photographing instantaneously of a scene* as viewed by the eye *and involved the following problems:*

*1. The pictures had to be taken from a single point of view and not from a changing point of view as with Muybridge and Marey. In other words, the camera should not move with respect to the background but the moving object or objects should move with respect to the camera — exactly the reverse of what had been done before. And taking the pictures from a single point of view meant the use of a single lens.*[23]

However, if synthetic motion was valued lowly by scientists themselves, it was used by journalists, writers and cultural commentators precisely to *praise* science. The cinema — and the science that lay behind it — at last enabled the prospect, if not the reality, of conquering death itself, the ravages of time, memory and decay:

> *Cinematography is not essentially something for fun, a toy for big children. By faithfully reproducing any kind or type of movement, it constitutes man's most astonishing victory to date over forgetfulness. It retains and restores the things memory alone can't recover, not to mention its auxiliary agencies: the written page, drawing, photography. This new addition to the treasure house of memories held in common, this resurrection of what appeared to be most fleeting in the escaping past, can and must serve mankind as have writing, printing, engraving, stenography.*
>
> *Like them, cinematography prevents the things of yesterday that are useful to tomorrow's progress from sinking into oblivion; amongst these one must count moving things, which only a few years ago were considered impossible to fix in an image. Surely, the importance of preserving them can't be denied.*[24]
>
> *The beauty of the invention resides in the novelty and ingenuity of the apparatus. When these apparatuses are made available to the public, everybody will be able to photograph those who are dear to them, no longer as static forms but with their movements, their actions, their familiar gestures, capturing the speech on their very lips. Then, death will no longer be absolute.*[25]
>
> *When at last colour photography has been achieved, and when a phonograph has been added to that, then movement and speech will be caught simultaneously, recorded simultaneously and reproduced simultaneously with rigorous accuracy, that is to say life itself. When that day has come — and it is coming tomorrow —*

23. Edison quoted in Richardson 'What Happened in the Beginning', pp. 23–4

24. Boleslas Matuszewska quoted in Jacques Deslandes and Jacques Richard, **Histoire Comparée du Cinéma**, vol. 2 (Paris: Casterman, 1968) p. 13

25. **La Poste**, 30 December 1895, quoted in Sadoul, **Louis Lumière**, p. 119

science will have given us the complete illusion of life. Why shouldn't it be capable of giving us life itself?[26]

The obsessive reiteration of this theme is not simply a product of nineteenth century hyperbole, or of its supreme, utopian, confidence in science. Nor is it solely because the century was obsessed with death — and with the myth that science could actually cheat, defeat or defy it. It is due also to the fact that the very motion which seemed to demonstrate life and memory, the final defeat of time, embodied also the workings of time, loss and death themselves:

*It is not by chance that Apollinaire's fascination with the new medium is immediately in 1907 the story of a murder, the relation of cinema and crime: film is exactly a putting to death, the demonstration of 'death at work' (Cocteau's 'la mort au travail'). Made of a series of stops in time, the timed stops of the discrete frames, film depends on that constant stopping for its possibility of reconstituting a moving reality — a reality which is thus, in the very moment of appearance on screen, as the frames succeed one another, perpetually flickered by the fading of its present presence, filled with the artifice of its continuity and coherence.*[27]

*The pictures shown are not only popular object-lessons in modern science, but they are charming in themselves, and for the images they evoke in the imagination. Sea-waves dash against a pier, or roll in and break languidly on the sandy beach, as in a dream; and the emotion produced upon the spectator is far more vivid than the real scene would be, because of the startling suddenness with which it is conjured up and changed, there in the theatre, by the magic wand of electricity. Street scenes, railway-trains in motion, boxing bouts, bull-fights and military evolutions are projected in life-like animations upon the luminous screen, while the audience sit spellbound in darkness . . .*[28]

Over and above the technology, on the one hand, and the films themselves, on the other, what was important, with the move toward cinema projection and the elaboration of the relations between spectator, projector and screen, was the experience of cinema, and the institutionalisation of that experience across society. It was this institutionalisation that rapidly came to determine the uses to which film technology would be put, to circumscribe what was technically and aesthetically possible.

26. **Le magasin pittoresque,** March 1895, quoted in Sadoul, **Louis Lumière,** p. 120

27. Stephen Heath, 'Film Performance', **Cine-Tracts,** vol. 1, no 2, Summer 1977, p. 8. The reference is to Apollinaire's short story '*Un beau film*', in which the perfect murder is committed by filming it and showing it to the public — nobody believes it is real

28. Henry Tyrrell, 'Some Music-Hall Moralities', in George C. Pratt (ed), **Spellbound in Darkness,** vol. 1 (New York: University School of Liberal and Applied Studies, 1966) p. 15

# The Cinematic Experience

The components of the cinematic experience, the elements comprising its socio-psychological specificity, have been discussed by Christian Metz, Jean-Louis Baudry, Julia Kristeva and others. Their discussions have turned precisely around those phrases used in Tyrrell's contemporary description quoted above: the dream-like status of film ('as in a dream'); the hyper-reality of the cinematic image ('more vivid than the real scene would be'); the spectator's position of contemplative fascination ('life-like animations upon the luminous screen, while the audience sit spellbound in darkness').[29] Rather than repeat those discussions here, it is important simply to stress that the experience that forms their subject lies at the heart of the social and historical significance of cinema and its technology. Capable though that technology was of producing other kinds of experience, other kinds of films (ones which emphasise, for example, the *disjunction* between the camera and human vision), it was the experience described by Tyrrell that effectively and massively prevailed, to be inscribed into the practices and products of what rapidly emerged as the cinema industry.

Emerging at the confluence of a disparate set of researches into optics and human vision, drawing upon the practices of popular theatre, music-hall, photography and academic and realist painting, dependent upon industrial technologies, expanding leisure time and, as a hypothesis, urbanisation that coincided almost exactly with the social multiplication of images and a social investment in the instance of vision, cinema secures its social and historical space precisely in so far as it offers and inscribes a new experience. It is this aspect and significance of cinema that is stressed in Jean-Louis Comolli's article, 'Machines of the Visible', and it is therefore with a quotation from this article that I would like to conclude this chapter:

*What happened with the invention of cinema? It was not sufficient that it be technically feasible, it was not sufficient that a camera, a projector, a strip of images be technically ready. Moreover, they were already there, more or less ready, more or less invented, a long time before the formal invention of cinema, 50 years before Edison and the Lumière brothers. It was necessary that something else be consituted, that something else be formed: the cinema machine, which is not essentially the camera, the film, the projector, which is not merely a combination of instruments, apparatuses, techniques. Which is a machine: a dispositif articulating between one another different sets — technological certainly,*

29. See Jean-Louis Baudry, 'Ideological Effects of the Basic Cinematographic Apparatus', **Film Quarterly,** vol. 28, no. 2, Winter 1974/5 and 'The Apparatus', **Camera Obscura,** no. 1, Fall 1976; Julia Kristeva, 'Ellipsis on Dread and the Specular Seduction', **Wide Angle,** vol. 3, no. 3, 1979; and Metz, 'The Imaginary Signifier'

*but also economic and ideological. A* dispositif *was required which implicate its motivations, which be the arrangement of demands, desires, fantasies, speculations* (in the two senses of commerce and the imaginary): *an arrangement which give apparatus and techniques a social status and function.*

The cinema is born immediately as a social machine, and thus not from the sole invention of its equipment but rather from the experimental supposition and verification, from the anticipation and confirmation of its social profitability; *economic, ideological and symbolic.*[30]

30. Jean-Louis Comolli, 'Machines of the Visible', in Heath and de Lauretis, **The Cinematic Apparatus,** pp. 121–2

# Part Two
# Sound

# 4:
## The Technology of Sound Recording

This section is concerned with the technology of sound in the cinema, more specifically with the history of its development and introduction, and with the economic, ideological and aesthetic determinants and effects that history involved. Detailed chronological accounts of the development of sound technology exist elsewhere.[1] What I want to do here is simply to give a sketch of that development before discussing the ways in which its various contexts both shaped and were in turn shaped by that development itself. Why did the technology of sound in the cinema develop as it did? Why was it adopted and sponsored by mainstream cinema at the particular time it was — rather than earlier or, indeed, later? What changes in the structures, institutions and experience of the cinema occurred as a result? Although detailed consideration is given primarily to the 1920s and early 1930s — the period which saw the introduction and consolidation of sound — a number of the more general points made later about the aesthetic effects of sound (the pleasures, meanings and experiences sound films involve) apply still, by and large, today.

1. Edward W. Kellog, 'History of Sound Motion Pictures', in Raymond Fielding (ed). **A Technological History of Motion Pictures and Television,** and 'The Technological Antecedents of the Coming of Sound', in Evan William Cameron (ed). **Sound and the Cinema** (New York: Redgrave Publishing Company, 1980) and Patrick Ogle, 'Development of Sound Systems: The Commercial Era', **Film Reader,** 2, January 1977

### Early Experiments

Sound consists essentially of variations of pressure in a given medium (like air) caused by a vibrating source and perceived through the ear by means of the ear drum (a membrane which itself vibrates as it comes into contact with the pressure waves). In the form of speech, song, music and noise, sound has been recorded and reproduced in a number of different ways. As far as the cinema is concerned the predominant means have been first sound-on-disc and secondly sound-on-film. Both means require a recording apparatus, a medium for storing the acoustic information thus recorded (a wax disc or celluloid film respectively), and an apparatus for reproducing that information. The history of the development and adoption of sound in the cinema involves the technology necessary to each of these three stages.

Efforts to record sound initially involved photography. Alexander Graham Bell, Professor E.W. Blake, Edmund Kuhn and others each tried to record photographically not just sound waves, but voice waves in particular. Prior to 1900, however, no

Edison Kinetophone

Amplifiers in place behind the screen

one had succeeded in reproducing the sound waves which had been photographed. Sound recording and sound reproduction had proved possible by other means, though, of which Edison's phonograph was one. It is well known, in fact, that Edison's initial experiments with a film camera and projector were motivated by the wish to devise a machine that 'would do for the eye what the phonograph does for the ear'.[2] He went on to build over fifty combination phonograph and peep-show machines.

The phonograph, in fact, provided the basis for most of the early attempts to combine recorded sound with film. Edison, for instance, went on to use the phonograph in a talking picture show that ran for several months at Keith's Colonial Theatre in New York in 1913. The phonograph was stationed behind the

2. Edison, quoted in Richardson, 'What Happened in the Beginning', p. 23

A sound on disc system

screen and linked to a synchronising mechanism on the projector by means of a string pulley running the length of the auditorium. Prior to that, Léon Gaumont in France and Carl Laemmle in America had experimented with a combination of phonograph and projected film, in 1901 and 1907 respectively. Gaumont, in fact, continued work on his project for a number of years. Laemmle used a German system called Synchroscope. It was abandoned because of a lack of supply of films. Other systems were devised by George Pomerade in 1907, E.H. Armet (1912-18) and William Bristol, who began work around 1917.

Edison's first sound apparatus

All the early phonograph systems reproduced sound accoustically. The needle in the disc or cylinder groove upon which the sound was stored transmitted its movements to a diaphragm. The vibrations of the diaphragm were then perceived by the ear as sound. The sound tended to be very faint, and was amplified by linking the diaphragm to a horn. Even so, there were limits to the volume of sound thus obtained, and amplification problems were accompanied by difficulties in obtaining a high fidelity in sound reproduction and in sustaining synchronisation between phonograph and projector, sound and image.

An earlier attempt at an amplification system

Amplification was improved enormously with the invention of the Audion tube by Lee De Forest in 1913, while work on sound-on-film systems was designed to solve the problems of synchronisation.

The Audion tube enabled sound to be amplified electronically. It thus contributed towards improvements not only in reproduction, but also in recording. Taken together with subsequent improvements and developments in its working and design, it provided the basis for much of the technology of sound in the cinema when it was eventually adopted by the industry on a large and permanent scale.

## Sound-on-Film

The basic technology involved in all sound-on-film systems entails the registration of sound-modulated light beams on to photographically sensitive film. The sound thus registered is then reproduced by means of a device which converts the light modulations into electronic modulations. These are then subsequently amplified and transformed into modulations of the air — sound waves. In early experiments with the recording of sound on film, a variety of light sources were tested for suitability: arc lamps, gas discharge tubes, oxyacetylene flames and gas flames among them. Attempts were also made to reflect sound-modulated light on to film by means of mirrors.

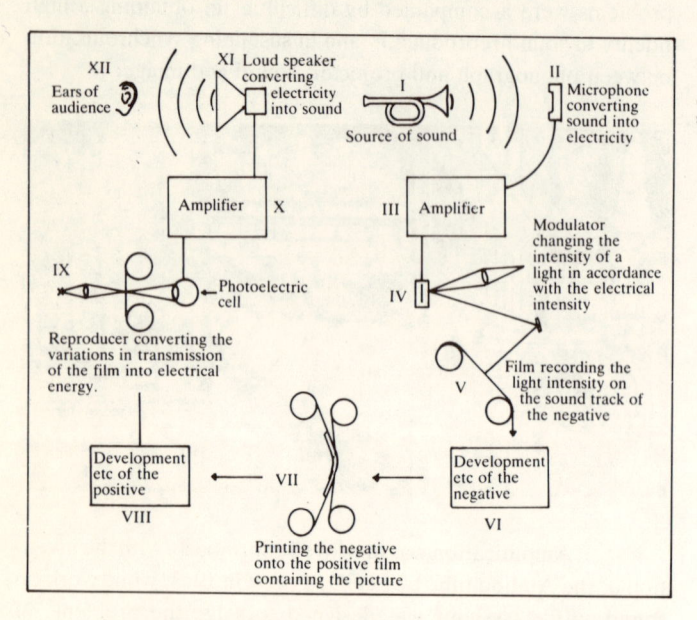

Cycle of operations in sound recording

Further attempts to record sound photographically were made by Ernst Rühmer and Eugene Lauste. Rühmer invented a photographic sound camera called the photographophone. Lauste's interest in photographic sound recording began while working with the Edison organisation in America in the 1880s. He secured a British patent on the idea of combining picture and

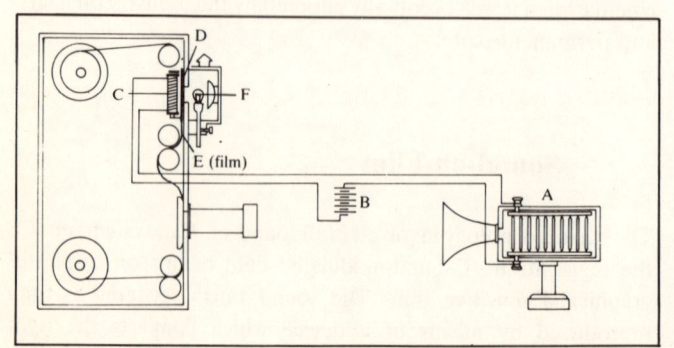

Diagram of Lauste's sound recording camera, 1906. Sounds picked up by the carbon rod microphone (A) were converted into variations of current supplied by the battery (B), causing the electromagnet (C) to vibrate a moving grid (D), through which light passed to the film (E) from an electric lamp (F). A variable density sound track was produced

sound on the same piece of film in 1907. He is believed to have realised this idea in practice in his Brixton studio in London in 1910. Lauste went to the United States to demonstrate his system, then came back to England, where lack of finance and the advent of the First World War combined to interrupt his research.

Working in the United States, Professor Joseph T. Tykociner at the University of Illinois had been interested in photographic sound recording since the turn of the century. Initially using a manometric gas flame as a light source (flames from a gas jet so arranged that sound modulations produced fluctuations in the gas supplied to the jet), he abandoned work for a time owing to the lack of electronic amplification and to the fact that he had to rely on the relatively insensitive selenium cell for sound reproduction. He returned to his researches in 1918, by which time the photoelectric cell had been developed by Professor Jakob Kunz, also at Illinois University. Mercury vapour lamps had become available for sound modulation, and refined vacuum tube amplifiers and oscillators had been produced for sound reproduction. By June 1922 he was in a position to demonstrate his Phonoactinion system to a professional audience:

> Tykociner's system, designed and constructed within a reported budget of less than $1000, was an interesting blend of the old and the new, making use of the newly available high frequency currents, photoelectricity, and thermionic amplifiers, yet also using the traditional carbon grain telephone transmitter for a microphone and a Magnavox loudspeaker with 'morning glory' horn for reproduction. The sound recorder was mounted on a Bell & Howell 'Professional' camera . . . Reproduction was accomplished by scanning the variable density sound track with a potassium on silver cathode photoelectric cell.[3]

3. Ogle, 'Development of Sound Systems', p. 199

Tykociner did not go on to develop his system any further. He neither patented his device nor later derived any profit from it. Meanwhile in Germany, Josef Engl, Joseph Massole and Hans Vogt began work together in 1918 toward the development of a sound-on-film system which they called Tri-Ergon, 'the work of three'. First appearing in 1922–3, the Tri-Ergon system involved the use of a recording lamp which transformed the vibrating electric current in the rhythm of the sound waves emitted by the sound source into a luminous patch on the film. A photoelectric cell was used for sound reproduction, and electronics for amplification. A specially developed microphone (the 'Kathodophone') and electrostatic loudspeakers were also involved. This system was later employed throughout Germany, and was the basis upon which the struggle took place for control of the European market, an issue to which I shall subsequently return.

At around the same time Peterson and Poulsen, two Danish engineers, developed a system which was later commercialised in Germany under the name of Tonfilm. The photographic sound record was made by means of an oscillograph, a small mirror mounted on a pair of conducting wires in a strong magnetic field. The Peterson and Poulsen process was marked by the fact that sound and image track were separate, thus requiring a double system projector and a means of synchronisation. It was also marked by the use of a selenium cell rather than the photoelectric cell, the reason apparently being that Tri-Ergon owned the patents on the use of the latter. This system was used for some years both by Gaumont in France and by British Acoustic Films in the United Kingdom.

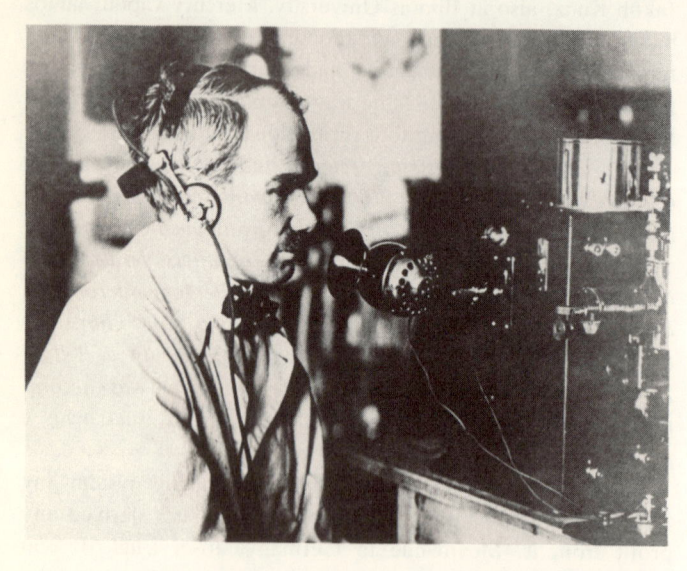

De Forest's phonofilm

Back in America, Lee de Forest was in 1923 able to announce and describe his 'Phonofilm' system, another process involving the use of sound on film. De Forest had invented the basis for electronic amplification, and sought in his system to avoid using any moving mechanical parts in microphones, light modulators and loudspeakers. As Patrick Ogle has noted, 'this purism on his part may have hindered his progress towards a commercially exploitable system'.[4] De Forest tried various light modulators until he settled on the 'Photion', 'a gas-filled tube excited by modulated high-frequency currents from a 5- to 10-w radio transmitter'.[5] While successful at recording, these tubes

4. Ogle, 'Development of Sound Systems', p. 200

5. Kellog, 'History of Sound Motion Pictures', p. 177

were limited in actinic light output; that is to say, they were not susceptible enough to chemical changes induced by light. Consequently, in 1922, de Forest entered into co-operation with the Theodore W. Case laboratory in order to make use of devices that Case had developed. De Forest was unable to interest established commercial producers in his system, in part because of a number of imperfections: 'insufficiently uniform film motion, limited frequency and volume range, loudspeakers that gave unnatural voices, and demonstration films that were probably rather uninteresting to all save their creators'.[6] De Forest was severely limited by lack of finance and financial backing. The Phonofilm system did begin commercial distribution in 1924. Some thirty theatres were wired to play it. In the end, however, lack of interest in the system on the part of the major commercial film companies, and lack of funds with which to pay for further research and development, meant that work on Phonofilm inevitably came to an end.

6. Ogle, 'Development of Sound Systems', p. 201

## Theodore Case and Movietone

Lee de Forest's relatively brief association with Theodore Case came at a time when Case himself had spent a number of years researching and developing a system for sound on film. Case became interested in deriving telephonic currents from modulated light while studying at Yale University in 1911. In 1914, he organised a laboratory in New York to study in particular those materials, like selenium, whose resistance is altered by light. This research resulted in 1917 in the development of the Thalofide cell, which involved the use of thallium oxysulfide as its photosensitive substance. The Thalofide cell was widely used in communications systems by the United States Navy during the latter part of the First World War, Navy sponsorship of the Case laboratories having provided the financial basis for much of Case's research during this period.

Case had been joined in 1916 by E.I. Sponable. Together they continued experiments into various aspects of audio communication, turning their attention in the early 1920s to the possibilities of developing a workable (and commercial) sound-on-film system. Work began in earnest in 1922. Manometric flames were initially tried as a source of modulated light. Soon after, however, Case found that light from one of his wartime argon arc signalling tubes was both readily susceptible to modulation and of high actinic power. A tube for sound recording called the Aeo-light was subsequently developed on the basis of these signalling tubes, helium being substituted for argon in 1922.

Case worked closely with de Forest from 1922 to 1925, each benefiting from the work previously and currently undertaken by the other. During this period, Earl Sponable designed and produced prototypes for a sound camera:

*The 1924 model was a modified Bell & Howell camera rebuilt to Sponable's specifications by the Bell & Howell Co. The film motion in this and other cameras was unacceptable until they had been reworked for greater mechanical precision. In the final designs of sound camera the sprocket was driven through a mechanical filter, consisting of damped springs and a flywheel on the sprocket shaft. The sound was recorded on the sprocket. The Aeo-light was mounted in a tube which entered the camera at the back.*

Once the working arrangement with de Forest came to an end in 1925, Case's efforts were directed towards the production of reproduction equipment. A 'sound head' was developed that could be attached to existing projectors. A small lamp illuminated the passing sound track, which was then scanned by a potassium photoelectric cell. The microphones, amplifiers and loudspeakers used in Case's system were manufactured by Western Electric, a giant corporation at this time itself involved in

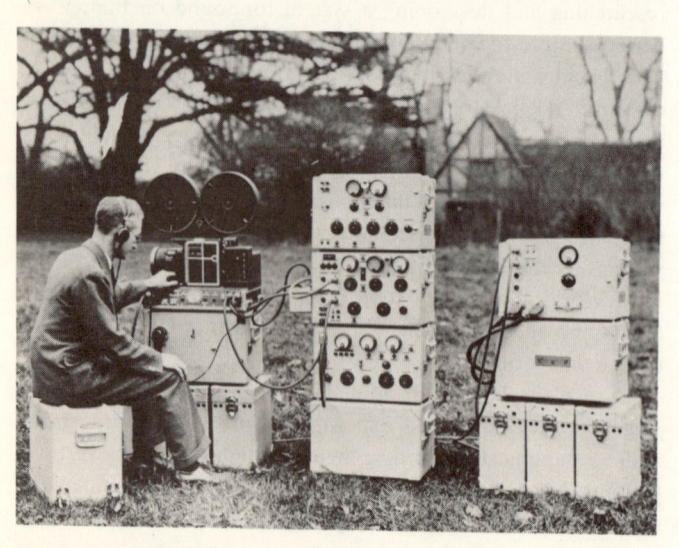

7. Kellog. 'History of Sound Motion Pictures'. p. 178

Western Electric recording channel in operation

the development of a sound film system. Case licensed this Western Electric equipment initially from Vitaphone (in 1926) and then subsequently from 1927 on from Electrical Research

Products Incorporated (ERPI), a subsidiary of Western Electric and the Bell Telephone Company.

Demonstrations of the Case sound system were held for representatives of the Fox Film Corporation and then for William Fox himself. This was early in 1926. On 26 July that year, an agreement was signed between Fox and Case according to which Case turned over all patents and rights to a new corporation, Fox-Case. The trade-name 'Movietone' was adopted for the system and a number of shorts (newsreels, vaudeville acts and the like) were filmed. These were premièred to the public at the Sam Harris Theatre in New York on 21 January 1927, at the première of a silent feature film, **What Price Glory?**

## Western Electric and Vitaphone

As noted above, Case's system dependended upon the use of microphones, amplifiers and loudspeakers produced by Western Electric. Indeed, they were used by almost all the commercially successful talking picture systems in the United States. Western Electric had acquired rights to the Audion in 1913 and worked from there to produce their amplifiers. Condenser microphones had been developed by Dr E.C. Wente in 1916. Loudspeaker improvements had come about as a result of the company's experience in public address and radio. These developments were at least in part a consequence of Western Electric's general research into the fields of sound and speech.

They were the primary equipment suppliers to the Bell Telephone Company and were involved in producing equipment for the sound recording and radio industries. It was in the period from the early to mid-1920s that Western Electric became involved in simultaneous research into both a sound-on-film and synchronised sound-on-disc systems for use in the field of cinema.

Sound-on-disc was in a sense a logical outcome, or rather a logical by-product, of Western Electric's work in the field of sound recording. A programme of research into the study of speech waves had been initiated in 1912, and soon spread to the study of music. Various improvements were initiated in sound reproduction for disc recordings and in amplification. After the war, a group of researchers under J.P. Maxwell undertook the development of improvements in wax recording and the phonograph, producing as a consequence a new magnetically driven disc cutter, and a newly improved phonograph called the Orthophonic. These improvements were then rapidly incorporated into synchronised sound and picture devices. Demonstrations of a successively improved process were given in 1922 and 1924.

The system worked as follows. In filming and recording, a marked frame was set in place in the camera gate while the recording stylus was set at a marked point on the record. A pair of selsyn motors linked through electrical connections provided the means of synchronisation between the motion picture camera and the disc cutter. The camera ran at a rate of 24 frames per second. The 400 foot magazines of film used in silent filming were replaced by magazines with a capacity of 100 feet, allowing takes up to eleven minutes long. Large, 16 inch discs rotating at 33⅓ revolutions per minute were needed to match these reels in recording time, the pick-up travelling from the centre of the disc to the outer edge.

For reproduction, the turntable and projector were geared mechanically together in order to ensure proper synchronisation. Each reel of film would be threaded in the projector with a marked frame aligned in the aperture. The accompanying disc was placed on the turntable with the stylus cued to the start mark. 'The sound information on the disc was scanned by means of a replaceable steel needle attached to an oil-damped electromagnetic pick-up which converted the oscillations of the stylus into feeble electric currents. These currents were in turn amplified and sent forth into the theatres by means of rather conventional Western Electric Public Address amplifiers and loudspeakers . . . placed behind or adjacent to the screen.'[8]

8. Ogle, 'Development of Sound Systems', p. 203

Vitaphone in operation

This was the system which came eventually to be known as Vitaphone. Numerous demonstrations were held for the major Hollywood production companies, but with little success. Eventually, Warner Bros. became interested in the system and its

Variety, 7 August 1926, regarding Vitaphone

commercial potential, and the Vitaphone corporation, with Samuel L. Warner as its president, was organised in April 1926 to exploit and to market the process Western Electric had developed. A feature film with post-dubbed music and sound effects, **Don Juan**, was released using Vitaphone in August 1926. Production of a second feature, **The Jazz Singer**, with Al Jolson, began in the spring of 1927 and was premièred in New York on 6 October that year:

> cumbersome and largely immovable though its sound recording system was, the Western Electric sound-on-disc Vitaphone system provided the first great commercial success for sound motion pictures . . .[9]

9. Ogle, 'Development of Sound Systems', p. 203

## Western Electric and Sound-on-Film

Concurrently with its sound-on-disc system, Western Electric worked also on producing a sound-on-film system, using the same microphones, amplifiers and loudspeakers.

Experiments at Western Electric in the photographic recording of sound using an oscillograph had begun, somewhat unsuccessfully, prior to the 1920s. Later experiments conducted by A.O. Rankine proved more successful, and in 1923 work began in earnest using the light valve as a means of recording. The valve, similar in principle to the one used earlier by Eugene Lauste, but operating with two ribbons rather than one, worked in conjunction with a set of lenses. The two ribbons 'rested in a strong magnetic field, with currents made to flow in the opposite directions in the ribbons so that they would deflect edgewise to increase or decrease their separation and so modulate the light passing through the slit'.[10]

10. Ogle, 'Development of Sound Systems', p. 206

Unlike the Movietone system, Western Electric's system used a sound recorder separate from the camera, the two being synchronised by means of selsyn motors. And where the camera used conventional negative film stock, the sound recording was made on positive film, which had a higher grain and was hence less susceptible to distortion, crackle and noise.

Once the separate sound and picture tracks had been printed and married together, the reproduction of sound and image was produced in a manner similar to that of the Movietone system, with a soundhead mounted on an adapted movie projector. A pre-amplifier was used to increase the level of output of the photocell scanning the sound track. This was so that the output from both the sound-on-film and the sound-on-disc systems would match one another, enabling the same amplifiers to be used in both systems.

## General Electric and Sound-on-Film

A different sound-on-film system was developed at General Electric, like Western Electric a major American corporation. Elements of the system were developed at Westinghouse. In October 1919, General Electric established The Radio Corporation of America (RCA) and transferred to it several radio and audio patents and agreements entered into by General Electric,

Westinghouse, the Wireless Specialty Company, the Radio Engineering Company of New York and American Telephone and Telegraph. RCA and its subsidiary, RCA Photophone Incorporated, acted as a sales outlet for the system that came to be developed and known as Photophone.

The system itself developed as a consequence of experiments conducted at General Electric in the field of telegraphic and radio communications. A photographic telegraph recorder for radio reception was developed by one of General Electric's engineers, Charles A. Hoxie, as a means of making a visual record of transoceanic radio signals on photosensitised paper. The signal 'vibrated a reed armature, which . . . imparted a rotary motion to a mirror, which caused a small spot of light to dance back and forth across the sensitive strip'.[11] This telegraphy recorder was then modified to record voice waves. Hoxie's first sound recorder was completed in 1921. A description of its principles is given by Edward Kellog:

*As in the case of the telegraph recorder, the track ran down the middle of the film, and was nearly an inch in width. In Hoxie's recording and reproducing machine the film was drawn over a physical slit on which intense light was concentrated. The width of the slit was about 0.001 in. Since an open slit would quickly fill with dirt, a wedge of fused quartz was ground to a thin edge and cemented in place between the metal edges which formed the slit. The face against which the film was to run was then lapped and polished. A photocell close behind the film picked up the transmitted light and an amplifier and loudspeaker completed the recording system.*[12]

A programme for the production of a commercial sound-on-film system, based on Hoxie's work, was initiated by General Electric in 1925. Like Hoxie's system, the sound track developed was to be of the variable area (rather than the variable density) type. A sound track encodes sonic information in the form of patches of light and dark on a strip of film. In a variable density system (of the kind developed by Case and by Western Electric) the sound information appears as gradations of black and white. In the variable area system, it appears as a wavy contour of black and white within the overall sound image. The variable area system had several advantages: 'it was less sensitive to the effects of improper exposure and development than variable density tracks, and was normally developed to a very high contrast, which was more in keeping with the processing of picture-bearing print positive film.'[13]

The basis of the variable area system at General Electric

11. Kellog, 'History of Sound Motion Pictures', p. 182

12. Kellog, 'History of Sound Motion Pictures', p. 182
13. Ogle, 'Development of Sound Systems', p. 207

was the Duddell oscillograph, a modified oscillograph working with a mirror suspended between a set of ribbons. Like Western Electric, General Electric used a separate machine for recording sound. The photocell reproducer and amplifiers used by General Electric were similar also to those of Western Electric, though there was a difference in loudspeakers: 'Whereas the design by Wente and Thuras for Western Electric used a large exponential horn . . . with a small throat leading out from a small-diameter coil-driven metal diaphragm (similar to most exterior public address loudspeakers), the initial design by Rice and Kellogg for General Electric involved a larger diameter freely suspended coil driven paper cone surrounded by a flat baffle (similar to those used in radio and television receivers today). These were the loudspeakers (banked in multiples on either side of the screen) that were used in the first commercial appearances of the General Electric system, called Kinegraphone, that was employed in a road-show version of Paramount's **Wings** in 1927'.[14]

14. Ogle, 'Development of Sound Systems', p. 208

The contribution of Westinghouse Electric and Manufacturing Company in Pittsburgh consisted of an adaptation of the Kerr cell to photographic recording. The Kerr cell contained nitrobenzene, which rotates the plane of polarization of a light beam when subjected to an electrical field. There were a number of problems with the cell (the necessity of high voltage, distortion resulting from the non-linear relation between voltage and transmitted light, and the fact that nitrobenzene absorbs photographically valuable blue light). These problems were resolved sufficiently to enable the production of practicable cells, their advantage being their extreme speed. It appears, however, that the use of the Kerr cell in practice was restricted almost entirely to the production of newsreels.

For the purposes of the co-ordination of production, marketing, design, research and development, the agreement mentioned above between General Electric, Westinghouse and RCA was eventually made. Manufacturing, research and development were the province of Westinghouse and General Electric. RCA functioned primarily as a sales outlet for the equipment produced.

# 5:

## Sound and the Film Industry

### The Contexts of Technical Research

The extent to which reference has been made to the major electrical combines during the course of the foregoing historical sketch is a reflection of their increasing importance in the development of the technology of sound in the cinema. It is also a reflection of the changing conditions of technological research and development in general. Although it is certainly not the case that the early inventors worked in isolation in their garrets while the later ones were all employees of giant corporate laboratories, it *is* true to say that there occurred a discernible shift in the financial and institutional contexts within which experiment and research took place. The electrical combines and professional laboratories could provide funds and equipment on a scale unavailable before. One has only to look at the cases of Lauste and de Forest in particular to realise the extent to which the absence of these conditions hindered the development of sound technology. Edward Kellog cites Merritt Crawford's claim that had it not been for 'very limited resources, and had electronic amplifiers been available to Lauste, commercialization of sound pictures might well have gotten started a decade before they actually did'.[1]

Other, often directly related factors need to be taken into consideration in any adequate account of the conditions that led to the introduction of sound into the cinema in the late 1920s. One of these factors was the First World War, which generated a good deal of research into communications technology (as can be

1. Kellog, 'History of Sound Motion Pictures', p. 177

seen in the example of Case). The war involved the systematic funding of research into communications technology, thus stimulating the development of corporate research programmes and the shift in the context of invention and development away from the individual scientist and his laboratory and further towards the kind of enterprise that Edison had pioneered, with links in a field of highly capitalised activity:

*During the World War great impetus was given to the invention and perfection of all methods of electrical communication. Invention ceased to be a matter of individual ingenuity, and became a scientific operation conducted in large, well-equipped laboratories and shops, where physicists, engineers, and chemists worked together to solve the riddles of electricity, atmosphere, metals, and gases. Such laboratories are owned by the corporations engaged in telephone, telegraph, and electrical industries, and the patents on devices invented or developed in them usually pass to the ownership of the corporations. The American Telephone and Telegraph Company and its subsidiaries, Western Electric Company, Electrical Research Productions, Inc., etc., owned many important patents before, and in the years since, this group of corporations had acquired many more.*[2]

2. Benjamin B. Hampton, **History of the American Film Industry** (New York: Dover, 1970) p. 376

At the end of the War, state funds for research ceased to be available, but the War and the funds had in the meantime stimulated research, and the growth and consolidation of corporate technological development, to an enormous extent.

Another factor pertaining to earlier experiments was, much more simply, the difficulty involved in synchronising sound on disc (or sound on phonograph) with separately projected film. Added to this was the problem of amplification, not resolved properly until the advent of electronic amplification. It was the combination of these two factors that proved so decisive. It was their solution that led to the possibilities of sound becoming a significant feature of the commercial cinema. And here, once again, we are led back to the importance of the electrical trusts, the professional laboratories, and their funds and expertise. But we are led also, and simultaneously, to the absence of facilities of this kind within the industry itself, and to the industry's general conservatism with respect to technological development in general and to sound technology in particular.

The industry lacked any kind of research programme and facilities. Had these facilities been available, and had sound figured as the object of sustained research, it is possible that the industry itself could have resolved the kinds of technical problems referred to above fairly early in its history. The early experiments in sound that were undertaken by Edison, Gaumont, Laemmle and others could have been much more systematically funded and pursued. This, in itself, would have presupposed a film industry different in organisation and practice from what actually existed at the time. In fact, the only work on sound pursued within the industry seems largely to have been undertaken as a consequence of individual enthusiasms. With the lack of funds and facilities for research on a larger scale, it is hardly surprising that these enthusiasms tended to be limited both in scope and in lasting results.

Allied to these factors was a basic resistance to the kind of technological innovation that sound would have involved. There were a variety of reasons for this, most of them ultimately economic and financial in nature.

## Costs and Profits

As most accounts of the history of sound in film have stressed, Western Electric and the others had considerable difficulty in persuading the industry to consider their systems. Indeed, the biggest firms consistently refused even to attend demonstrations. As Douglas Gomery has shown, sound only entered the industry because Warner Bros. at that time were engaged in a programme of enormous expansion and investment, designed to put them up among the ranks of the major companies.[3] These companies had themselves invested considerable sums during the course of the 1920s in acquiring theatres, stars, directors and other assets: 'All were too profitable and had added too much capital in recent years to attempt such a risky investment'.[4] The adoption of sound would have required completely re-equipping studios and theatres; the adoption of new shooting and directing techniques; risking stars and actors untried in anything other than silent screen acting; and the abandonment of an aesthetic that had proved both popular and profitable. And over and above all these reasons was Hollywood's fear of losing the hegemonic position *vis-à-vis* the rest of the world which it had acquired during the First World War. Language difficulties alone were enough to deter it.

Some of these fears were, in a sense, to prove justified. The costs involved in adopting sound were huge. According to Alexander Walker, 24 million dollars were spent in reshaping the studios in the eight months prior to February 1929.[5] An estimated

3. J. Douglas Gomery, 'Writing the History of the American Film Industry — Warner Brothers and Sound', **Screen**, vol. 17, no. 1, Spring 1976
4. J. Douglas Gomery, 'The "Warner–Vitaphone Peril": The American Film Industry Reacts to the Innovation of Sound', **Journal of the University Film Association**, vol. XXVIII, no. 1, Winter 1976, p. 11

5. Alexander Walker, **The Shattered Silents** (London: Elm Tree Books, 1978) p. 124

300 million dollars were spent on theatres, amplification systems and recording apparatus.[6] A number of stars and actors proved unsuitable or unpopular in sound films. And because sound films were shot at a rate of 24 rather than 16 frames per second, and because in the first sound films scenes were shot with several cameras rolling at once, the costs of film stock per unit of screen time rose considerably. But while these costs served, among other factors, to reduce the number of independent producers and exhibitors, and while they obviously inflated the costs of production, the profits from sound films were enormous. Moreover, over and above the profits that very soon accrued to Fox, Warners and the other majors, there were additional savings and financial benefits.

Sound was originally envisaged as enabling the uniform production and reproduction of musical accompaniment to features and shorts. Many of the earliest sound films were simply audio-visual recordings of vaudeville acts, orchestras and opera singers. Many felt that the future for sound films lay here, in the provision for all cinema-goers of recordings of the best acts, performers and musicians:

> *inhabitants of small and remote places . . . will have an opportunity of listening to and seeing grand opera as it is given in New York.*[7]

At a time when it was common practice, certainly in the big, metropolitan cinemas, to precede the main feature film with music and vaudeville, and to accompany the film itself with live orchestral music, the implications of recorded music and recorded vaudeville acts were easy to see. On the one hand, costs could be cut, and on the other expensive acts and orchestras could be seen and heard cheaply throughout the country. As **Variety** pointed out in reviewing one of the earliest vaudeville shorts, packed with expensive stars, there 'were mighty few theatres in the land that could stand a tab as enormous as that'.[8] The estimated weekly wage bill for those stars featured in the shorts amounted to some 23,000 dollars.[9] In addition to savings on the cost of musicians' labour, there were profits to be made from the publishing and recording of music — especially from musicals. Fox became involved with De Sylva, Brown and Henderson, MGM bought up the Robbins Music Corporation, Warner Bros. bought Witmarks Incorporated, Paramount started the Famous Music Corporation, and so on. And there were further savings, at least initially, on actors' salaries. When sound was introduced, the number of scenes and takes was greatly reduced: dialogue tended to lengthen the scenes, and several cameras recorded each scene simul-

6. Walker, **The Shattered Silents**, p. 124

7. Mordaunt Hall, **The New York Times**, 7 August 1926, quoted in Walker, **The Shattered Silents**, p. 11

8. Quoted in Walker, **The Shattered Silents**, p. 16

9. Walker, **The Shattered Silents**, p. 16

taneously. Consequently, actors were employed for fewer days per film, thus reducing the costs of their labour:

> Photographic work on a silent film of standard length in 1925–6 may have averaged eight to ten weeks, while the average stars made four to six pictures a year. Standard sound films went through the studios in two to six weeks of camera time. The average players might get two to three weeks work in the silent, and a week to ten days in the sound, a reduction of one-third or one-quarter in days of employment.[10]

10. Hampton, **History of the American Film Industry**, pp. 398–9

## The Impact of Sound on the Structure of the Industry

The coming of sound precipitated a series of shifts and alterations within the film industry both nationally and internationally. It also produced a new and closer set of relations between the industry overall and other institutions: the electrical companies and trusts, the banks and other sources of finance capital.

First, the coming of sound saw the consolidation and expansion of vertical integration within the film industry in a number of different countries, the corporate integration of the three main branches of the industry: production, distribution and exhibition. Simultaneously, and most notably in America, it produced changes in the structure of relations between the different companies, a re-ranking, so to speak. A new structure emerged which was to last some twenty-five years. Vertical integration had begun in America with the race to acquire theatres and theatre circuits after the First World War, a result of the entry into the industry of First National, an exhibitors' circuit, and of the increasing importance to producers and distributors alike of the revenue derived from a film's first run. Throughout the 1920s, Paramount, Fox, Goldwyn Pictures, Loew's and others embarked on a programme of integration, expansion and, above all, the acquisition of first-run theatres. It was partly in order to counter the domination of these major companies, with their allied theatre chains, that Warners acquired sound. Having already acquired a distribution outlet through the purchase of Vitagraph, Warners decided to opt for further expansion through the smaller exhibitors and circuits, since they lacked a major theatre circuit of their own:

*The bulk of Warners' business was done with small independent circuits and struggling neighbourhood houses. If Warner could equip these theatres with sound, they could compete with the opulent downtown movie palaces. Sound, in the form of synchronized musical accompaniment for pictures, could provide a cheaper equivalent to live, full-sized pit orchestras. What Warner decided to do then was to produce entertainment programs for smaller exhibitors comparable in quality to those presented by the best metropolitan theaters.*[11]

11. Ballio (ed.), **The American Film Industry**, pp. 116–7

The success of sound allowed Warners to consolidate and expand, and to take its place among the majors. In September 1928 it purchased the Stanley theatre chain and one-third interest in First National. By the end of 1930, it controlled all of First National and boasted assets worth 230 million dollars.

Fox, likewise, used the profits sound provided to expand:

*Fox Film and its theatre properties, here called Fox Theatres, were nearly equal in size by 1925. By the end of 1929, Fox Film's assets had quadrupled and Fox Theatre sextupled. Profits had grown even more. With combined assets of almost $250 million, and profits of over $16 million, only Paramount remained larger.*[12]

12. Douglas Gomery, 'Problems in Film History: How Fox Innovated Sound', **Quarterly Review of Film Studies**, vol. 1, no 3, August 1976, p. 318

Fox, indeed, almost succeeded in creating and maintaining what would have been the biggest cinema empire in existence when it acquired the Loew family's share of Loew's Incorporated in 1928:

*The Fox-Loew's combination became the largest in the motion picture industry, surpassing even Paramount. The new company had assets of over $200 million, and an annual earnings potential of $20 million. It controlled over 800 theatres in the best locations. This takeover surpassed in both size and scope the creation of RKO, and Warner Bros.' acquisition of Stanley and First National. It was the largest in industry history.*[13]

13. Gomery 'Problems in Film History', p. 325. Fox was eventually unable to meet his short term debts following the Wall Street crash and had to relinquish ownership of Loew's in 1930

RKO (Radio–Keith–Orpheum), referred to in the preceding quotation, was formed in October 1928 by the Radio Corporation of America as a holding company, merging together Joseph Kennedy's Film Booking Office, the Keith-Albee-Orpheum circuit of vaudeville houses and Photophone. RKO was thus from the outset a vertically integrated giant, with four studios, 300 theatres and some $80 million of working capital.

Once sound had made an appearance, the established film companies acted cautiously. They signed an agreement to act together. The signatories, Loew's, Universal, First National, Paramount and Producers Distributing Corporation already occupied a substantial position in the industry and were already involved in integrated affiliations. Once sound had proved successful, and a particular system, Movietone, was adopted by the signatories, a further rash of mergers and expansions ensued:

*Adolph Zukor . . . added more theaters, bringing Paramount's total to almost one thousand in 1929. He also acquired a 49 per cent interest in the Columbia Broadcasting System. Then, in the fall of 1929, he proposed a merger with Warner Bros. that would create a motion picture and entertainment complex even larger than the Fox–Loew's combination and RCA combined.*

[Wadill] *Catchings and Harry Warner were agreeable, but the new US attorney general, William D. Mitchell, raised the red flag. If that merger went through, the industry would have been dominated by three firms. As it happened, though, it was to be dominated by five . . . The oligopolistic structure of the industry was now set, formed by Warner Bros., Paramount, Fox, Loew's, and RKO.*[14]

14. J. Douglas Gomery, 'The Coming of the Talkies: Invention, Innovation and Diffusion', in Ballio (ed.), **The American Film Industry**, p. 210

## Sound and the Industry in Europe

In Germany, a measure of cartelisation, concentration, and vertical integration was introduced with the formation of UFA in 1917. The Tri-Ergon sound system, once introduced, became the focus for further developments in this direction within the context of the international market and of struggles between Germany and the USA for European adoption of their respective sound systems and for the enormous profits they would bring. In 1928, the Tonbild Syndicate A.G. (Tobis), with the backing of capital from Holland, Switzerland and Germany, acquired the Tri-Ergon patents and began to install sound equipment in German cinemas. At the same time, the two giant German electrical firms, Siemens and Allgemeine Elektrizitäts Gesellschaft (AEG) produced their own jointly-developed system and formed Klangfilm. Tobis and Klangfilm united in anticipation of a struggle with the American companies and their sound systems, Tobis making the films, and Klangfilm the sound apparatus. Then Tobis signed an agreement with the Dutch firm, NV Kuchenmeisters Internationale Ultraphon Mij, centred in Holland, but with a production centre in Germany. A new company, NV Kuchenmeisters Internationale Mij voor Sprekende Films was formed, to which Tobis apportioned a third of its capital. With the Tobis–Klangfilm agreement still in force, the result was a huge, German-based, multi-national trust, Tobis–Klangfilm–Kuchenmeister. When an agreement was subsequently signed with UFA, control of the German film industry by a small group of companies was complete.

In France and Britain, concentration and vertical integration were similarly precipitated and accelerated by the coming of sound. In their case, though, this stemmed not from the ownership of sound patents enabling international expansion, nor from long-term corporate policies. It was dictated instead simply by the need to stem the influence of German and American firms.

In France, two large combines were formed, each with their own circuits of exhibition, distribution agencies, studios and laboratories: Pathé–Natan–Cinéromans and Gaumont–Aubert–Franco Films. These combines were the first to acquire sound equipment and techology in France.

In Britain, British companies sought to some extent to counter America (and Western Electric's draconian financial demands for the installation and use of their equipment) by turning to Germany. Tobis–Küchenmeister and British Talking Picture Corporation, for example, together founded Associated Ltd in 1929. But RCA then founded the Associated Radio Pictures Company with Associated, while Fox, through the Metropolitan and Bradford Trust, held capital in Gaumont British Pictures. By the early 1930s, Gaumont British and Associated British were the two large vertically-integrated combines which were to dominate the British industry at that time. Gaumont British was an amalgamation of Gaumont, the Ideal Renting Company, and W. & F. Film Service Ltd. It controlled eight circuits, owned Shepherd's Bush studios and also controlled Gainsborough Pictures. Associated British, originally registered as a private company, went public in 1927. Primarily a holding company, Associated British owned the entire capital of Associated British (with over 290 cinemas), British International (with its studio at Elstree) and the distribution units of Pathé Pictures and Wardour Films.

## Finance Capital and the Coming of Sound

In addition to the acceleration of vertical integration and the tendency toward the formation of large, often multi-national combines and trusts, the coming of sound saw a consolidation and extension of relations between the film industry, the giant electrical trusts who owned the sound systems and patents, and the various institutions of finance capital. These institutions provided the film industry with money for converting to sound and generally played an important part in financing the electrical trusts themselves.

In America, banks, insurance companies and Wall Street in general had already become involved in the film industry in the early to mid-1920s, when the various companies were seeking expansion through the acquisition of theatres. In 1919, Kuhn, Loeb and Company and associated bankers had been instrumental in selling a 10 million dollar issue of preferred shares in the Paramount-Lasky Corporation as part of Adolph Zukor's plans to acquire theatres in the face of competition from First National. Other links with other firms soon followed. The John F. Dryden-Prudential Insurance group backed Fox. Goldwyn was financed by Dupont and the Chase Manhattan Bank. Loew's had affiliations through board membership with General Motors and the Liberty National Bank. Universal was backed by Shields and Company, the investment bankers. And so on. According to Alexander Walker banks during the period 1926–8 had been 'buying into the film industry to the tune of 500 million dollars'.[15] 'By the start of 1929,' he writes, 'over 40 banking and electrical company presidents sat on the boards of the largest film companies.'[16] The enormous costs involved in converting to sound generated the need for huge sums of ready capital, so the industry turned to the financial institutions for money. Those institutions and their representatives, meanwhile, were in part responsible, through their advice, for encouraging expansion and hence the adoption of sound in the first place. Warners and Fox, for example, both acquired sound on the basis of advice from the financial institutions which had undertaken to back them, Goldman, Sachs in the case of Warners and Halsey, Stuart and Company in the case of Fox. The effect, if not the intention, was an increase in the influence of financial institutions such as these, an increase in the dependence of the film companies upon them, and closer links between the industry and Wall Street in general.

Financial capital was fundamental too to the giant electrical corporations involved in the development of sound. Western Electric was a subsidiary of A.T. & T. General Electric, through its involvement in the formation of RCA, came under the influence of Rockefeller's interests when in 1930 RCA passed into the hands of the Chase National Bank. The following diagrams, from F.D. Klingender and Stuart Legg's **The Money Behind the**

15. Walker, **The Shattered Silents**, p. 46
16. Walker, **The Shattered Silents**, p. 125

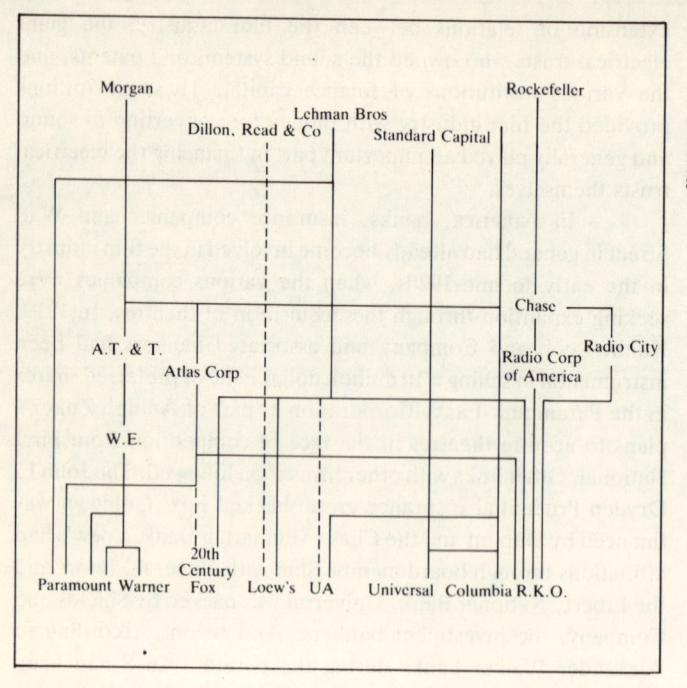

Direct financial control of Hollywood. From F.D. Klingender and S. Legg, **The Money Behind the Screen**, p. 74

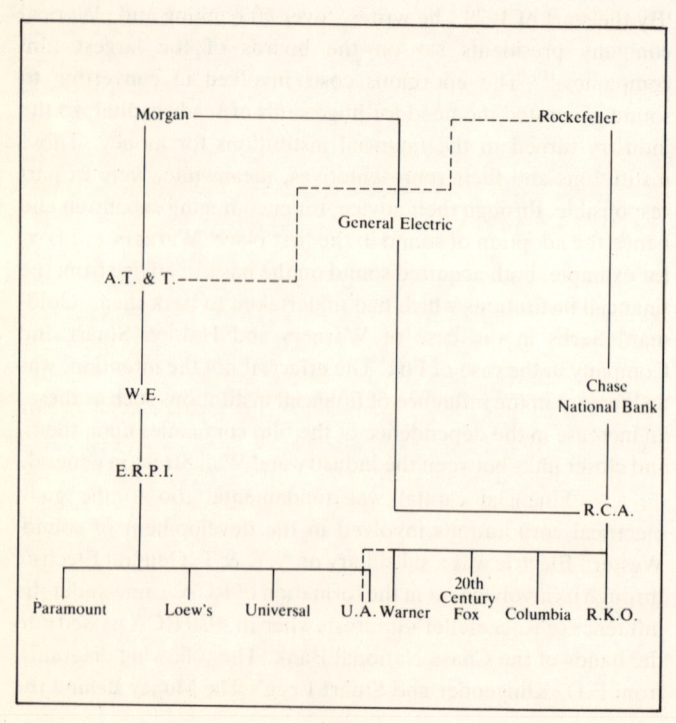

Indirect financial control of Hollywood. From F.D. Klingender and S. Legg, **The Money Behind the Screen**, p. 70

Screen,[17] give a simplified picture of the extent of the interrelations between the film industry, the electrical trusts, finance capital in general, and the financial interests of Morgan and Rockefeller in particular during the mid-1930s. By this time the power of the financial institutions had been further augmented by the Depression, when many of the major film companies were forced to reorganise following a period of huge financial losses and even bankruptcy.[18]

A similar process of involvement of finance capital occurred in the German, French and British film industries. In Germany, the role of the banks was particularly important. Farben had links with Tri-Ergon and Tobis with the Commerz und Privat Bank. As has already been mentioned, the Tobis–Klangfilm–Küchenmeister combine eventually involved financial backing not only from Germany, but also from Holland and, earlier, Switzerland. In France, Pathé–Natan–Cinéromans was sponsored by Bauer and Marshall, Gaumont–Aubert–Franco Films by banks in both Switzerland and France. In Britain, Gaumont-British involved capital from the Metropolis and Bradford Trust Company, while according to Klingender and Legg, major creditors to the industry as a whole included the National Provincial Bank, the Equity and Law Life Assurance Society and Prudential Assurance.

## Further Changes in the Industry's Structure and Practice

The coming of sound involved and precipitated a further series of shifts and changes in the structure and practice of the film industry. These shifts and changes are in themselves fairly heterogeneous. They can all be linked, however, to the adoption of sound; and while sound itself did not directly 'cause' them all, they all, equally, can be viewed as direct or indirect effects of its adoption.

First, there were changes in film rental practice and in the mode of employment of labour. Before the coming of sound, most films rented for a flat fee. However, since revenues from silent films could not be used as a guide for charges on sound films, distributors started to charge a percentage of box-office revenues, with a minimum guarantee, instead of an outright flat fee:

*The major producer-distributors would share in the excess profits if a film did well and be protected if it did not.*

---

17. F.D. Klingender and Stuart Legg, **The Money Behind the Screen** (London: Lawrence & Wishart, 1937) pp. 70 and 74

18. For short, succinct accounts, see Ballio (ed.) **The American Film Industry**, pp. 214–6 and Conant, **Antitrust in the Motion Picture Industry**, pp. 29–32

*Independent exhibitors vigorously protested for they did not wish to expose their accounts to constant surveillance by the majors. Still these independent exhibitors gave in quickly; they did not want to lose access to the highly profitable 'talkies'. Producer-distributors then hired checkers to monitor audience size to guarantee accurate accounting.*[19]

With regard to labour and employment, the advent of the talkies coincided with a shift from freelance to contracts. This, in turn, can be seen as part of a process of standardisation that affected industry labour relations as much as its processes of production.

Here, everything was transformed. Studio laboratories were re-organised and automated. Developing and printing procedures were standardised. 'Every aspect of timing had to be standardised. Hand-cranking disappeared and editing, previously done by eye and hand, was standardised by the introduction of the moviola.'[20] There were changes, too, in the 'look' of the films. Carbon arc lights, which hummed and were thus useless for filming with sound, were replaced by tungsten lights, which were at the red end of the spectrum. So the old orthochromatic film stock, which was blind to red, was replaced by panchromatic stock, which although available earlier on, had not been extensively used. Similar problems in sound control led to the adoption of studio rather than location-based shooting, as the norm for outdoor as well as indoor scenes. This, in turn, facilitated the development of background projection techniques.[21]

The coming of sound also saw the final establishment of the feature film, rather than shorts or accompanying stage and musical acts, as the main attraction for cinema-goers. In the major cinemas, the replacement of live entertainment by sound films involved a clear and substantial saving in labour costs. For the smaller cinemas, such savings were appreciably less substantial. From the point of view of the electrical companies selling sound equipment, therefore, it was crucial that the feature film itself be the prime focus of attention and attraction, and that the sound feature replace the silent feature in popularity. And this, in fact, is what happened. In addition, there were changes in exhibition practice and the customs and habits of viewing, stemming from the nature of sound films themselves. Films were now viewed in conditions of quiet and much more as entities, to be seen (and heard) from beginning to end:

*Harold B. Franklin said in his 1929 manual of instruction for theatre-owners that the dialogue picture would enforce prompter public attention from the start of a picture since 'if the*

19. Gomery, 'Hollywood Converts to Sound: Chaos or Order?', p. 28

20. Wollen, 'Cinema and Technology: a Historical Overview', p. 17

21. For further details concerning film stock, the adoption of the moviola and the development of back projection see Barry Salt, 'Film Style and Technology in the Thirties', **Film Quarterly,** Fall 1976

*motion-picture follows the construction in playwriting, the earlier part of the action . . . will establish the premise for the action that is to come.'* He advised making special trailers enforcing silence on patrons before the show began.[22]

22. Walker, **The Shattered Silents**, p. 99

Here, of course, we begin to touch upon the crucial impact of sound upon the nature of the films themselves, upon the nature of the film viewing experience, and upon the nature of meanings and pleasures produced and engaged by mainstream cinema.

# 6:

# Sound and Film Aesthetics

## Sound in Silent Cinema

Perhaps the first and most obvious effect of the advent of sound was the standardisation, through mechanical and electronic recording and reproduction, of the aural address of mainstream film. As has often been pointed out, silent films were, in fact, rarely seen in conditions of silence. They were variously accompanied not only by the noise of the projector and the audience, but also by the spoken commentary of a 'master of ceremonies', by music, sound effects, and by dialogue and commentary spoken live by professional actors. As Raymond Fielding insists, 'there was never any such thing as a silent film — at least as far as the audiences were concerned'.[1] Fielding goes on to elaborate on some of the components involved in the aural address of silent films. Music was provided not only by pianos and organs but often — increasingly — by orchestras:

*With the introduction of more elaborate theaters devoted exclusively to the exhibition of the motion pictures, and the financial growth of the industry, special scores were oftentimes produced by composers and arrangers for particular films, the various movements, phrases, and melodies being scored in appropriate order and tempo so as to insure a reasonable synchronism between the live music and the projected images. The use of such custom-made scores, beginning at least as early as 1908, represented the first widespread system for pre-determining and guaranteeing a particular sound and image relationship from performance to performance and from theater to theater.*[2]

1. Raymond Fielding, 'The Technological Antecedents of the Coming of Sound: An Introduction', in Cameron, **Sound and the Cinema**, pp. 3–4

2. Fielding, 'The Technological Antecedents of the Coming of Sound', p. 4

Sound effects, too, were introduced early, becoming more regular and more mechanical as the industry and its films developed:

> *Some of these were generated by elaborate organs or special effects machines such as the Noiseograph, the Dramagraph, the Kinematophone, the Soundograph, and the excelsior Sound Effect Cabinet.*[3]

The role of the master of ceremonies was an interesting one. Analogous, as Fielding points out, to the Japanese *benshi*, the master of cermonies added a dimension to the structure of address involved in silent film, his voice oscillating between its function as an extension of the film itself (speaking the characters' dialogue, generally amplifying the drama of the story) and its role as a source of information and authority outside it (perhaps giving technical information about the film and those involved in its production). Fielding highlights the variety of functions he performed:

> *First, as a conventional master of ceremonies, he provided a link between the new and somewhat disreputable motion picture and the more respectable music hall and vaudeville traditions with which audiences were familiar. Second, he read the sub-titles, which were then, as they are today, crucial in introducing abstract ideas of any intellectual complexity into the silent motion picture experience. This was an especially important service for those members of the audience who either could not read English or could not read at all. Finally, he interpreted the motion picture experience artistically for the members of the audience — a crucial contribution at a time when the form and structure of the film, particularly insofar as it involved changes in camera position or editing, was likely to confuse audiences.*[4]

Finally, there were the actors, hired to stand behind the screen and to read or improvise dialogue in some kind of synchronisation with the actors on screen:

> *The systematic use of such live performers during motion picture presentations began at least as early as 1897 with the work of the entrepreneur Lyman H. Howe, and during the first decade of the century a number of professional actors companies were founded to provide such services to theaters on a regular basis. These included the Humonova, Actologue, and Dramatone companies.*[5]

Noting in a number of these instances the increasing move toward standardisation (the use of specially composed and arranged scores, the use of standard acting companies) and/or mechanisation (the use of noise machines and organs equipped to

3. Fielding, 'The Technological Antecedents of the Coming of Sound', p. 4

4. Fielding, 'The Technological Antecedents of the Coming of Sound', p. 5

5. Fielding, 'The Technological Antecedents of the Coming of Sound', p. 5

produce standard special effects), the point to stress about the coming of sound-on-disc and, even more evidently, sound-on-film, is that they standardised and mechanised the aural component in film to an extent hitherto impossible.

In fact, then, the *'silent film' is a myth. It never existed.* Furthermore, the term was rarely used prior to 1926 — only afterwards . . .

What was introduced in 1926 was an entirely different kind of sound, permanently recorded by technological means in a single, particular version for each particular film, and reproduced so that exactly the same sound performance accompanied that film from day to day, theater to theater, screening to screening. Furthermore, it was intended that these sounds would be precisely synchronised with particular actions which occurred on the screen. Most notably, this applied to dialogue, but in just as significant a manner it applied to music and sound effects as well.[6]

In so far as standardisation and mechanisation were qualitatively increased, in so far as synchronisation was increased and, just as importantly, in so far as sound was now much more closely identified with the screen and the film itself, the coming of sound was not simply an extension or culmination of a set of developments with regard to the use and practice of sound with film, it was simultaneously a consolidation and transformation of them. Sound opened up new possibilities and developments just as it definitively changed a number of aspects of films and the viewing of films. In order to identify these changes it is worth initially taking a closer look at 'silent' films.

6. Fielding, 'The Technological Antecedents of the Coming of Sound', pp. 5–6

## Characteristics of Silent Cinema

In many ways, and much more obviously than was the case with the talkies, silent cinema was in a constant process of change and development. The first twenty to twenty-five years saw constant evolution, especially as regards the development of cinematic narration, lighting and *mise-en-scène*.[7] Nevertheless, if we take the silent cinema of the late teens and early 1920s as a rough model, and if we bear in mind the common factor of the absence of complete, standardised and synchronised sound, dialogue and music, a number of general points and observations can be made. First, there was a distinct and different form of audience attention:

7. On the development of cinematic narration, and, consequently, the development of conventions in the relationship between film and spectator, see Noel Burch's film **Correction Please (Or How We Got Into Pictures)**, Arts Council of Great Britain, and Barry Salt, 'The Early Development of Film Form', **Film Form**, Vol. 1, no. 1, Spring 1976. On lighting, see Peter Baxter, 'On the History and Ideology of Film Lighting', **Screen**, vol. 16, no. 3, Autumn 1975

> *The addition of dialogue did not simply add a dimension to the experience: it replaced an attitude towards it. It shattered the emotional communion between the silent movie and its audience: it was rather like what had been happening on the film sets. Silent movies had enabled the casual customer to drop in, and within a minute or two be locked into the story and characters. Mime-acting made the characters' predicaments easily intelligible: sub-titles gave people emotional cues to follow rather than narrative points to recall. But dialogue altered all this: it demanded attention, it enforced silence on the audiences who had hitherto been able to swap comments on the movie below the music of the pianist or pit orchestra. Now one had to shut up, sit up and pay attention to a plot that more and more was conveyed in words, not pictures.*[8]

Especially in the later and longer silent films, much initial time was devoted to exposition: the introduction of characters (and actors), the delineation of the narrative situation and its relevant fictional history and, on occasion, the specification of the moral themes to be elaborated and pursued. With the absence of sustained aural dialogue, with the absence of the voice, there was a different use of and emphasis on acting, titles, lighting, décor and image:

> *The absent voice re-emerges in gestures and the contortions of the face — it is spread over the body of the actor. The uncanny effect of the silent film in the era of sound is in part linked to the separation, by means of intertitles, of an actor's speech from the image of his/her body.*[9]

> *the silent cinema makes up for its lack of sound by displaying its codes and conventional devices, by using intertitles to convey words (thus breaking iconic continuity and consequently disturbing narrative flow), and by elaborating a system of significations keyed to an emphatically gestural and corporeal mode of expression.*[10]

The use of sub-titles meant a separation between actor, title and spectator: instead of the voice of the actor filling and fleshing out the enunciation of the dialogue, the dialogue was instead silently fleshed out by the spectator, then projected back on to the figure of the actor. In the absence of the recording of the actor's voice, a voice was provided by each spectator individually:

> *Each spectator brings his personal enunciatory code, and the intertitle provides merely the matrix of the statement to be produced.*[11]

None of this is to claim that silent cinema was in any sense more 'progressive' than sound cinema, that the degree of

8. Walker, **The Shattered Silents**, p. 97

9. Mary Ann Doane, 'The Voice in the Cinema: The Articulation of Body and Space', **Yale French Studies**, no. 60, 1980, p. 33

10. Daniel Percheron, 'Sound in Cinema and its Relationship to Image and Diegesis', **Yale French Studies**, no. 60, 1980, p. 17

11. Michel Marie, 'Muet', **Lectures du Film** (Paris: Albatross, 1975) pp. 170

stylisation it involved, for example, meant that it was in and of itself aesthetically radical. What it *is* true to say is that the aesthetics of silent film, and in consequence the mode of spectatorship it involved, were both distinct and different. The coming of sound produced real changes in the mode and address of narrative cinema.

## The Aesthetic and Experience of Sound Film

The introduction of sound allowed the synchronisation of dialogue with the image of the actor (and with the image, so to speak, of the actor's voice). It contributed both to a decisive orientation of space, time and narrative around individualised characters and to a rigid codification of cinematic story-telling according to the conventions of what has come to be termed 'classical *découpage*'. *Découpage,* in this context, refers to a whole nexus of conventions relating to the cinematic articulation of time and space within and between shots, sequences, segments and scenes. These conventions include all the various forms of match-cutting (eye-line matches, direction matches, the 180 degree rule, and so on).[12] They also include the varieties of cinematic and narrative point of view,[13] and, less specifically cinematic, the systematisation of the modulated scene — the building of a scene such that information is picked up from a previous scene, developed and expanded, then left such that further scenes are built upon the information it itself provides; the modulated scene is marked by a particular economy of repetition and variation, by the necessity for a certain degree of screen time — much more than is required by the more impressionistic, segmented and elliptical narrative style characteristic of modern Hollywood films — and by the need for dialogue: the interaction and exchange of information among and between a set of characters.[14] Finally, classical *découpage* is marked by, and dependent upon, individualised speech and dialogue and individualised characterisation. It was the integration of rapidly developed conventions and rules for shooting and editing dialogue (the use of shot and counter-shot in conjunction with a 'continuous' sound track of speech and dialogue) into a system of conventions governing the articulation of narrative space and time, together with the degree of 'presence' and psychological individualisation provided by the voice, that finally completed the evolution of the conventions of narrative film.

12. For an elaboration on these forms, see Noel Burch, **To the Distant Observer**, pp. 2–3
13. See Edward Branigan, 'Formal Permutations of the Point-of-View Shot', **Screen**, vol. 16, no. 3, Autumn 1975
14. See Raymond Bellour, 'The Obvious and the Code', **Screen**, vol. 15, no. 4, Winter 1974/5

These conventions, together with the embellishments and modifications enabled by the use of the long take and depth of field, were to remain the foundation of narrative cinema.

It was in part the development of these conventions that was to be taken as a hallmark of the cinema's new capacity for realism. Films now were closer in the way they told their stories to the novels of the nineteenth century, the very touchstones of realist art. Added to this, and as part and parcel of it, was the simple fact that with the addition of sound, mechanically or electronically reproduced, the cinema could now reflect more of the world as experienced through our two basic senses:

*Film with sound and speech will provide the most marvellous reproduction of life as it unfolds before our eyes.*[15]

Realism doubly guaranteed, by approximation to the conventions of the novel and by the technological reproduction of sounds as well as sights.

It is at this point important to stress the extent to which sound and the sound track are subject to construction, are as much the product of rules and conventions as the perspective image, on the one hand, and the complete and complex narrative on the other. Mechanically and electronically reproduced and synchronised sound introduced, in theory, a wide range of aesthetic possibilities and practices. Given the aesthetic, economic and industrial contexts in which sound was introduced, however, those possibilities, in practice, were rapidly curtailed. The conventions of classical *découpage* became the norm, came to dominate the production of sound films almost totally after a very limited period of confusion and experiment. So at this fundamental level sound in cinema is conventional, not natural, 'realist' but not real.

But not only is sound a selection from available possibilities, it is also a construction. As Alan Williams has argued, there is no such thing as sound 'in itself'. Sound 'is a three-dimensional, material event'.[16] It is never independent of its environment, nor of the position and perspective of the person who hears it. If this is the case,

*then it follows that sound recording can not by definition reproduce 'sounds in themselves' — since it is obligated by its nature to render a sound (as vibrating volume) as recorded from one point of the space in which and through which the sound exists.*[17]

What we hear in a recording is thus never the original sound, 'but one perspective on it, a *sample*, a *reading* of it'.[18] Thus

*in sound recording, as in image recording, the apparatus performs a significant perceptual work for us* — *isolating, inten-*

15. **Filma,** no. 260 9/11/29. Quoted in Roger Icart, L'Avènement du Film', **Les Cahiers de la Cinémathèque,** 13–15, 1975, p. 103

16. Alan Williams, 'Is Sound Recording Like a Language?', **Yale French Studies,** no. 60, 1980, p. 53

17. Williams, 'Is Sound Recording Like a Language?', p. 53

18. Williams, 'Is Sound Recording Like a Language?', p. 53

*sifying,* analyzing *sonic and visual material. It gives an implied physical perspective on image and sound source, though not the full, material context of everyday vision or hearing, but the* signs of *such a physical situation.*[19]

In addition to this process of selection, sampling, reading and construction there is then a whole panoply of convention and practice governing the treatment of the sound recorded in its relations with the image and with the overall mode of signification into which that sound is inserted. Thus, to take an obvious example, within the realist conventions adopted by Hollywood during its classical period, sound perspective would be carefully related to image perspective. If a character were seen speaking in close-up, his or her words would be heard as if speaking in close-up, as it were, and not as if speaking from the back of a large hall. Hence sound, once recorded, is subject to further manipulation: 'all manipulations possible in image recording have analogs in sound. There are sound edits, for example, as well as dissolves, super-impositions and so on'.[20] Sound is generally recorded within specific frequencies in accordance with distinct ideological rules:

*The human ear hears on average frequencies between 30 and 16,000 cycles. The transposition of optical sound to cinema filters out any sounds above 10,000 cycles. The norms for the low/high scale were fixed in Hollywood in 1932 on the basis of a pleasant sound that corresponded, according to opinion polls, to the taste of an 'average individual' in the United States in the 30s (according to Michel Fano). Cinematographic sound is still founded on that standardisation.*[21]

During the processes both of mixing and recording, the sound track is then further manipulated such that individual sounds and specific types and forms of sound are stratified and subject to the establishment of a hierarchy in which dialogue and speech are accorded, overall, a primary role:

*Mixing, as does any work in an auditorium, requires specialised and expensive equipment, which explains why these operations have been very standardised and severely restrict the possibility of any initiative that goes beyond the norms consecrated by dominant usage. Sounds are rigorously apportioned in terms of the primacy of speech and its maximum audibility. There exists a hierarchy in sounds which it is difficult to transgress. The characteristic work of mixing is that of unification, homogenisation, the softening and smoothing out of any 'harshness' in the sound.*[22]

The predominant practices of recording and mixing thus

---

19. Williams, 'Is Sound Recording Like a Language?', p. 58

20. Williams, 'Is Sound Recording Like a Language?', p. 60

21. Claude Baiblé, Michel Marie, Marie-Claire Ropars, **Muriel** (Paris: Editions Galilée, 1974) footnote, p. 66

22. Michel Marie, 'Son' in **Lectures du Film**, p. 203

work both to intelligibly stratify, unify and homogenise the sounds recorded, pulling them into a single fictional space, and to accord primacy within that space to the human voice, speech and dialogue. The

> sound-track corresponds to the reunification of different heterogeneous sound-tracks, emanating from diverse sources in the process of fabricating filmic sound.[23]

23. Marie, 'Son', p. 203

In producing that stratification and unity, and in according the voice that primacy, these practices then feed into the further process of the combination of sound and image, the construction of the audio-visual fiction. And it is here that the possibilities of synchronisation become crucial, the key term of that synchronisation then being the matching of speaker and speech, actor and voice, dialogue and the image of its enunciation:

> Dialogue is given primary consideration and its level generally determines the levels of sound effects and music. Dialogue is the only sound which remains with the image throughout the production — it is edited together with the image and it is in this editing that synchronisation receives its imprimatur *as a neutral technique through the sanction of the moviola, the synchronizer, the flatbed.*[24]

All the forms of sound involved in a sound track are matched to the image in one way or another (including, of course, the music, though the matching here is not generally determined by the need to synchronise it with the image of its production). However, given the role of speech within the hierarchy of sounds, it is the matching of speech and dialogue that is crucial:

24. Mary Ann Doane, 'Ideology and the Practice of Sound Editing and Mixing', in Heath and de Lauretis, **The Cinematic Apparatus,** p. 52

> there is no doubt that synchronisation (in the form of 'lip-synch') has played a major role in the dominant narrative cinema. Technology standardizes the relation through the development of the synchronizer, the moviola, the flatbed editing table.[25]

The importance of 'lip-synch' is determined not just by the importance of dialogue within the classical fiction film and its system of narrative. It is determined also and simultaneously by the fact that 'lip-synch' functions as the pivotal point in relation to which systems of on-screen and off-screen, diegetic and extra- or non-diegtic sound are established,[26] and most importantly, through which sound overall is identified with, and subordinated to, the image.

25. Mary Ann Doane, 'The Voice in the Cinema: The Articulation of Body and Space', **Yale French Studies,** no. 60, 1980, p. 34

26. For discussion and analysis of these various systems, see Percheron, 'Sound in Cinema and its Relationship to Image and Diegesis'. With respect to the articulation of music within these systems, see Claudia Gorbman, 'Narrative Film Music', **Yale French Studies,** no. 60, 1980

Owing to the various forms of manipulation to which it must necessarily be subject in order to produce the types of hierarchical mixing discussed above, the sound track must first of all be separate (separated from) the image. However, once those manipulations have taken place, the two must be married together, and in such a way as to establish the primacy of image and vision. These fundamental practices, and the conventions to which they are subject, were established very early on, when there was a specific problem involved in recording music and speech together (owing to the difficulties of balancing the two types of sound if they were both recorded by the same apparatus simultaneously):

> The industry's solution to this problem, already generally operational by late 1929, was to record the music separately — in an atmosphere conducive to proper music recording — then to play the recorded *music back while the scene was being acted and its dialogue recorded. This so-called 'playback' system had the immediate effect of separating the sound track from the image — a primary factor in the constitution of film ideology. By facilitating the matching of a performer with a sound which he had not necessarily created, the playback permitted immediate capitalization on the sound film's fundamental lie: the implication that sound is produced by the image when in fact it remains independent of it.*[27]

This 'lie' is achieved fundamentally by the filming of people talking: synchronisation is visually re-marked while the source of the sound (and its paradigm, speech) is marked and anchored by the image of the speaking actor:

> *Perhaps the single most important difference between silent and sound narrative films lies in the latter's increased proportion of scenes devoted to people talking — devoted, that is, to moving lips.*
>
> *The more we expose the importance of dialogue in narrative cinema, however, the less comprehensible becomes the practice of pointing the camera at the person talking. If it is the dialogue, the language, the words which count, then why show lips moving in time with the sound track? We can best answer this question by recognising the effect of those moving lips: they transfer the origin of the words, as perceived by the spectator/auditor, from sound 'track' and loudspeaker to a character within the film's diegesis. To put it another way, pointing the camera at the speaker disguises the source of the words, dissembling the work of production and technology.*[28]

Sound and image are homogenised, unified, bound together across the 'body' of a single text, a single 'space' of meaning and perception. Sound is anchored to the image, to the space and time it depicts, and this is further reinforced by the spatial arrangement of the cinema itself, with the loudspeaker positioned behind the screen, the source of the sound further identified with the space of the image and the fiction itself. All this

27. Rick Altman, 'Introduction', **Yale French Studies**, no. 60, 1980, p. 6

28. Rick Altman, 'Moving Lips: Cinema as Ventriloquism', **Yale French Studies**, no. 60, 1980, p. 69

so as to unify, to contain, not just the filmic text itself, not just the space of the auditorium, but also the senses and psyche of the viewer:

> *The placement of the speaker behind the screen simply confirms the fact that the cinematic apparatus is designed to promote the impression of a homogeneous space — the sense of the fantasmatic body cannot be split. The screen is the space where the image is deployed while the theater as a whole is the space of the deployment of sound. Yet, the screen is given precedence over the acoustical space of the theater — the screen is posited as the site of the spectacle's unfolding and all sounds must emanate from it.*[29]

It is the spectator — the viewer, and listener — who is the ultimate point of address of these practices, arrangements and conventions in the use of sound introduced, almost simultaneously, with the new sound technology itself. If sound meant a certain reorientation in the address of the cinema to its audience, a certain reorientation in the conventions of cinematic story-telling, it meant also, as part of these processes, a new relationship between spectator and text and, as part of that relationship, the necessity to engage and to entertain a new drive, a new form and source of pleasure: the drive to listen or hear; the pleasure of sound and the voice.

Just as the image and its composition and articulation in narrative film involves and intensifies the desire to look, the pleasure of the gaze, so the technical and aesthetic practices evolved rapidly around the new technology of sound involve and intensify the 'invocatory drive', the desire to listen, to hear. First, as Jean-Louis Comolli has pointed out, the primacy accorded the effect of a pleasant and easily intelligible clarity in the recording and mixing of sound generally and dialogue in particular contributed simultaneously to an abolition, so to speak, of the distance between listener and sound, and to the constitution of the listener as eavesdropper, aural voyeur, almost co-present with the actors on the screen, yet invisible, unseen and unheard:

> *Why is it that the intelligiblity of dialogue is so important a technical problem, demanding so much care and attention on the part of the sound engineer? It is not simply in order that the dialogue be clearly understood by the spectator, it is also, more interestingly, for reasons relating to the co-presence of the characters and the spectator. In fact, the intelligibility of the dialogue allows these words and voices to be heard as though one were there with them; there is a direct interpellation of the spectator who is set on the stage on which the dialogue takes place. What is interesting is the way in which this completely abolishes both the technical*

29. Mary Ann Doane, 'The Voice in the Cinema: The Articulation of Body and Space', p. 38: 'the body reconstituted by the technology and practices of the cinema is a *fantasmatic* body.' (pp. 33–4)

*mediations that are what precisely render possible this kind of dialogue* in absentia, *which is the typical dialogue of representation, and, equally, the real space-time of any communication, a communication always being simultaneously mediated and disturbed by space-time — as I speak to you, for example, my voice is involved in a certain effort to reach you, there is a work of the body against the resistance of the matter of space, air and so on. All this is abolished in the dominant system of Hollywood representation so as to give the impression of a co-presence, a coexistence of the spectator and the characters on the screen.*[30]

The spectator — as both spectator *and listener* — is positioned as 'invisible guest', as someone who '*overhears* and, overhearing, is unheard and unseen himself'.[31] Sound, dialogue and music are recorded, mixed, manipulated and integrated into the system of the film and its narration so as precisely to structure and intensify that position, hence the drives and pleasures it involves and maintains. It is surely no accident, then, that one of the genres so central to the early sound period was the musical, a genre precisely designed, as it were, to render sound spectacular. In articulating sound as music and voice as song, the musical intensifies as far as possible the drives and the pleasures of listening. (Within one short ten-month period in 1929, Hollywood released films like **Broadway Melody, Hearts of Dixie, Hollywood Revue, Show Boat, On With the Show, Desert Song, Hallelujah,**

30. Jean-Louis Comolli, Intervention, in Heath and de Lauretis, **The Cinematic Apparatus**, p. 57

31. Doane, 'The Voice in the Cinema', p. 43

**Broadway Melody** (Harry Beaumont, 1929). *Courtesy MGM–UA*

Rio Rita, Sunny Side Up and Show of Shows. In Germany, at the same time, films like Liebeswaltzer, Drei von der Tangstelle, Hungarian Rhapsody, The Congress Dances and other 'Viennese Operettas' were being produced.)

The Congress Dances
(Erich Charell, 1931)

## Psychology, Pleasure and Sound

Mary Ann Doane, drawing extensively upon the work of the French psychoanalyst Guy Rosolato, has discussed these drives and desires and their articulation within mainstream cinema at some length.[32] It is worth finally closing this chapter on sound by repeating the salient points in her article, and by adding one or two further remarks, comments and hypotheses.

32. Doane, 'The Voice in the Cinema', especially pp. 43–6

    Psychoanalysis situates pleasure — and desire — in the gaps between an initial experience of need fulfilled, the marks established by that experience, future repetitions of those marks or signs and future attempts to repeat the experience itself. Pleasure and desire are hence founded in an urge to repeat. Within this broad and general framework, one can locate the pleasures and desires of listening within memories of the first experiences of the voice. On the one hand, the voice is endowed with the power to demand (the voice of the child is used to command attention, to signify its various needs). On the other it can function as the very sign of bodily unity (sound is simultaneously emitted and heard by the child itself, while the voice of the mother 'is a major component of the "sonorous envelope"

33. Doane, 'The Voice in the Cinema', p. 44
34. Doane, 'The Voice in the Cinema', p. 44
35. Doane, 'The Voice in the Cinema', pp. 44–5

which surrounds the child and is the first model of auditory pleasure'.)[33] As the instrument of demand the voice 'appears to lend itself to hallucination, in particular the hallucination of power over space',[34] while an 'image of corporeal unity is derived from the realization that the production of sound by the voice and its audition coincide. The imaginary fusion of the child with the mother is supported by the recognition of common traits characterizing the different voices and, more particularly, of their potential for harmony . . . the voice makes appeal to the nostalgia for an imaginary cohesion . . .'.[35] In this context, it is surely no accident that two films which deal specifically, though very differently, with what one might term 'aural voyeurism', Claudia Alemann's **Blind Spot** and Francis Ford Coppola's **The Conversation,** both evoke heavily Oedipal themes centred around the

Gene Hackman in **The Conversation** (Francis Ford Coppola, 1974). *Courtesy Paramount Pictures Corporation*

Gene Hackman in **The Conversation** (Francis Ford Coppola, 1974). *Courtesy Paramount Pictures Corporation*

mother and the 'primal scene' and both conclude with the central protagonist playing musical instruments — a violin and saxophone respectively. The playing of these instruments is in both cases the mark of a wish for 'imaginary cohesion', ultimately for a nostalgic fusion with the mother.

The voice also, however, is later associated with difference, division and language:

*the imaginary unity associated with the earliest experience of the voice is broken by the premonition of difference, division, effected by the intervention of the voice of the father . . . The voice in this instance, far from being the narcissistic measure of harmony, is the voice of interdiction. The voice thus understood is an interface of imaginary and symbolic, pulling at once towards the signifying organization of language and its reduction of the range of vocal sounds it binds and codifies, and towards original and imaginary attachments.*[36]

36. Doane, 'The Voice in the Cinema', p. 45

The voice thus lies at the intersection between narcissistic and nostalgic drives and desires, and the differential networks of language, together with the functions or organisation, meaning and authority with which it can be invested.

The forms and practices of sound recording and reproduction discussed above tend to locate the address of mainstream sound films within an ambit both of narcissism and nostalgia and of a clarity and identity of meaning. These forms and practices thus tend

> *to sustain the narcissistic pleasure derived from the image of a certain unity, cohesion and, hence, an identity grounded by the spectator's fantasmatic relation to his/her body. The aural illusion of position constructed by the approximation of sound perspective and by techniques which spatialize the voice and endow it with 'presence' guarantees the singularity and stability of a point of audition, thus holding at bay the potential trauma of dispersal, dismemberment, difference. The subordination of the voice to the screen as the site of the spectacle's unfolding makes vision and hearing work together in manufacturing the 'hallucination' of a fully sensory world.*[37]

In order that this be achieved,

> *the potential aggressivity of the voice ... must be attenuated. The formal perfection of sound recording in the cinema consists in reducing not only the noise of the apparatus but any 'grating' noise which is not 'pleasing to the ear'. On another level, the aggressivity of the filmic voice can be linked to the fact that sound is directed* at *the spectator – necessitating, in the fiction film, its deflection through dialogue (which the spectator is given only obliquely, to overhear) and, in the documentary, its mediation by the content of the image.*[38]

One might add that developments in sound techology since the 1930s, notably the introduction of magnetic and stereo sound tracks in the 1950s and, more recently, the introduction of Dolby, merely serve to reinforce this thesis, aimed as they are both at increasing the 'spectacle' of sound and at complementing the 'formal perfection of sound recording'.

These hallmarks of aural address in sound films can perhaps help, finally, in pinpointing the importance of the coming of sound with respect to the characteristics of the aural address in silent cinema. The latter, marked as it was by the use of a master of ceremonies, of musical accompaniment, and of sound effects was characterised by a spatial heterogeneity in its sources of sound, albeit that all the tendencies in their deployment were towards standardisation and unification. These tendencies could only go so far. The pianist, organist or orchestra could be located

37. Doane, 'The Voice in the Cinema', pp. 45–6

38. Doane, 'The Voice in the Cinema', p. 46

Laying the sound track for **Apocalypse Now** (Francis Ford Coppola, 1979)

just in front of the scene, the master of ceremonies beside it, the actors speaking dialogue behind it. But the identification of sound with image and screen could never be so complete as it became with the coming of sound films.

# Part Three
# Colour

# 7:

## The Technology of Colour Photography

The final section of this book is concerned with a description of the various technologies of colour cinematography that have played a part in the history of mainstream cinema, with an analysis of some of the different economic and institutional bases that provided the conditions for the emergence of these technologies, and the aesthetic and ideological determinants and effects those technologies have had both in theory and in practice. Starting with a brief description of the scientific basis of colour photography and cinematography, I shall go on to give an account of some of the technologies and colour systems that have been developed during the course of the cinema's history (concentrating in particular on Technicolor, whose role in mainstream cinema since the 1930s has been notably hegemonic), seeking to emphasise the economic, ideological and aesthetic factors that influenced their development. Finally, I shall be concerned to emphasise the extent to which the ideologies of colour cinematography and its use in film have been formulated in terms of the themes of women, nature and beauty, the extent to which, in theory and in practice, the development and description of the spectacle of colour in film has been centred around the image of the female body as the focus simultaneously of nature, artifice, beauty and the look.

# The Nature of Colour

Colour, very basically, is the mental or psychological result of the physical action of different light waves on our eyes and optical nervous system. Light itself consists of radiant energy of distinct and different wavelengths. The wavelengths in total form the spectrum of light — that range of radiant energy which the human eye can perceive. The eye and the optic nervous system overall form a specialised apparatus for responding to this range of radiant energy. When we perceive an object as being of a particular colour, this perception is the result of two distinct processes. First, it is the result of the modification of light by the object itself, which, in accordance with its own physical properties, will reflect some elements of the spectrum of light that strikes it and absorb others. Secondly, it is the result of the physical and psychological characteristics of the perceiving subject and its optical apparatus.

Light is made up, then, of different wavelengths of energy which we perceive as different colours. Objects are perceived as being differently coloured in so far as they absorb and reflect different colours in the spectrum. A red ball, for instance, is a ball which reflects the red light in the spectrum and which absorbs most or all of the other colours. For each of the different colours in the spectrum there have been found to be three key or 'primary' colours — red, green and blue. Mixtures of these primary colours can produce all the other colours in the spectrum, and when added together, they produce white. Conversely, when any one of the three primaries is subtracted from white, the result is a light composed of the other two. Colour can thus be produced by the subtraction as well as the addition of the three primary components of white light. It is this property of light

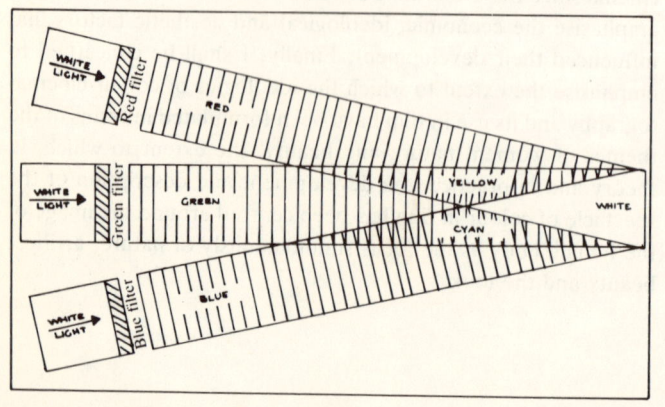

Diagram of additive colour process, showing mixture of three primary colours producing white light

and of the three primary colours, and the theory that accounts for it, that forms the basis of the two main methods, or, rather, categories of method, that have been used to produce colour photographically in film: the additive method, and the subtractive method. The additive method works by adding together the primary lights, starting, as it were, with no light at all. The subtractive method begins with white light (i.e. a combination of all the different visible rays) and subtracts from it various proportions of the three primary colours.

## Colour and Photography in the Nineteenth Century

As part and parcel not only of the massive investment in growth of the natural sciences during the nineteenth century, but also and in particular of that regime of spectacle and that especially intense focus on the properties and limitations of vision and the human eye referred to earlier in the book, the theories of colour, light and vision that underlay the development of colour in photography (itself part of that regime) were produced primarily during the 1800s. Following Isaac Newton's experiments with the prism and the spectrum, and the publication of his theories of colour in 1704, work on colour was produced and developed by Young, von Hemholtz and Maxwell. In 1801, Thomas Young proposed a theory that the retina in the eye contains three sets of nerve fibres, each receptive to one of the three primary colours. In 1855, a Scottish physicist, James Clerk Maxwell illustrated the implications of Young's theory with reference to photography, thereby laying the foundations of colour photography itself:

> Let it be required to ascertain the colours of a landscape by means of impressions taken on a preparation equally sensitive to rays of every colour. Let a plate of red glass be placed before the camera, and an impression taken. The positive of this will be transparent wherever the red light has been abundant in the landscape, and opaque where it has been wanting. Let it now be put in a magic lantern along with the red glass, and a red picture will be thrown on the screen. Let this operation be repeated with a green and a violet glass, and by means of the three magic lanterns let the three images be superimposed on the screen. The colour at any point on the screen will then depend on that of the corresponding point on the landscape and . . . a complete copy of the landscape . . . will be thrown on the screen.[1]

1. Maxwell, quoted in Brian Coe, **Colour Photography, The First 100 Years 1840–1940** (London: Ash & Grant, 1978) p. 28

On 17 May 1861, Maxwell gave a practical demonstration at the Royal Institution in London. He made three still photographs of an object — one through a green filter, one through a red filter, one through a blue — then projected the positives through a triple lens lantern slide, each screened through the appropriate filter, thus rebuilding, as it were, the object's original colours:

*Three photographs of a coloured riband, taken through the three coloured solutions respectively, were introduced into the camera,* [i.e. the projector] *giving images representing the red, the green and the blue parts separately, as they would be seen by each of Young's three sets of nerves separately. When these were superimposed, a coloured image of the riband was seen, which, if the red and green images had been as fully photographed as the blue, would have been a truly coloured image of the riband. By finding photographic materials more sensitive to the less refrangible rays, the representation of the colours of objects might be greatly improved.*[2]

Maxwell's method was an additive method, a variation on which was proposed by Ducos du Hauron in a French patent in 1868 and in his book **Les Couleurs en Photographie,** published in 1869. His proposal was for a screen made up of fine lines of red, yellow and blue which when viewed from a distance could not be resolved individually.

*By selectively blocking the lines of the screen any colour could be produced. For example, blocking the yellow lines would allow only red and blue light to pass through, giving purple, while covering the yellow and red lines would allow only blue to pass through.*[3]

The screen was placed in front of the film in the camera, resulting in an image of minutely coloured lines. Dots could be used instead of lines, and the principle behind du Hauron's proposal, that of using a mosaic, so to speak, of coloured filters, was the principle behind the subsequently developed 'lenticular' processes, in which the colour filters, in the form of dots or lines, were present in the film base itself.

Du Hauron also outlined the initial ideas and principles behind subtractive colour processes. These processes are dependent on the fact that each of the three primary colours has its own 'complementary' colour: cyan for red, magenta for green and yellow for blue. Each complementary absorbs or subtracts the primary to which it corresponds. It is, as it were, its opposite. Cyan absorbs or subtracts red; magenta absorbs or subtracts green; and yellow absorbs or subtracts blue. By superimposition,

2. Maxwell quoted in Coe, **Colour Photography,** p. 28

3. Coe, **Colour Photography,** p. 46

the three complementaries can thus produce all the other colours. Red is produced by superimposing magenta and yellow, green by superimposing cyan and yellow, and blue by superimposing cyan and magenta. According to Brian Coe, du Hauron's proposal was as follows:

> that three negatives be made up of the same subject, by orange light, green light and violet light. Three positives could then be made from them, printed on semi-transparent paper 'prepared with the complementary colours'. The orange record was printed in cyan (blue-green), the green record in magenta (blue-red) and the violet exposure in yellow (a red-green mixture). When the three positives were carefully superimposed, a full colour reproduction would result. Each of the three complementary colours absorbs or subtracts one of the primary colours. Thus, a cyan image, depending on its density, will vary the amount of red light passing through it, performing the same function as the black and white image and red filter of the additive process. Similarly, the magenta filter controls the green light passing through it, and the yellow image the blue. By superimposing them, the three colours will produce all the others.[4]

4. Coe, **Colour Photography**, pp. 84–5

The subtractive processes work, then, on the principle of subtracting various proportions of the three primary colours from white light. They are each subtracted by the three complementaries. Each complementary thus subtracts its primary, while reflecting or transmitting the remaining two-thirds of the spectrum. The processes involve two distinct stages. In the first stage, original exposures are made through red, green and blue filters on to negative film. Remembering that the light values on negative film are the opposite of what they are on positive (black appears white and vice versa), the next stage is to print a positive whose colour values are thus as it were the opposite of those on the negatives. Thus the red filter negative is printed as cyan, the green as magenta and the blue as yellow. The resulting positive transparency then acts as a three-colour filter when placed between the eye and a source of white light, and the result is a full colour image representing the colour values inherent in the object or scene initially photographed. This is the common principle behind subtractive colour processes, though the details, methods and techniques of both of the two stages vary (and have varied) from process to process.

# Early Colour Processes in Film

The earliest patent for what, significantly, have come to be called 'natural' colour processes in film (processes in which the colour is produced photographically) was awarded in 1897 to H. Isensee of Berlin for an additive process. By 1900, several colour systems were in existence, the additive McDonagh system, for example, and the subtractive Sanger–Shepherd process. Between then and the introduction and consolidation first of the Technicolor two-colour process and then of the Technicolor three-colour system in the 1930s and 1940s, numerous colour systems, both additive and subtractive, were developed either in theory or in practice. None proved to be commercially successful or viable for more than a few years, and relatively few films were made or released commercially in any of these processes. This is not to say, however, that colour did not play an important part in film and in what might be termed cinema's regime of representation prior to the introduction and success of Technicolor. Far from it. From the facts and figures available it would seem that a substantial part of the industry's output was coloured in one way or another, through the processes of hand-painting, stencilling, tinting or toning the prints. R.T. Ryan for example, has claimed that by the early 1920s, 'during some periods 80 to 90 per cent of the total production was printed on tinted positive film'.[5] Similar figures are quoted by James Limbacher.[6] Before going on, then, to outline one or two of the important cinematographic colour processes, and to discuss some of the reasons for their relative lack of commercial stability, penetration and success, it is worth taking a look at these other methods and techniques of producing colour in film.

5. R.T. Ryan, **A History of Motion Picture Colour Technology** (London: Focal Press, 1977) p. 16
6. James Limbacher, **Four Aspects of the Film** (New York: Brussell and Brussell, 1969) p. 12

The very first colour films, Edison's **Annabell's Butterfly Dance,** Paul's **The Miracle,** much of the work of Meliès, and others, were all coloured by hand. Each of the frames were individually painted or tinted. The length of the films, on average something like fifty feet, plus the cheapness of the labour involved, plus the limited number of copies made, were the conditions that together made what would otherwise seem a laborious and expensive technique feasible:

*Motion pictures in colour could be seen in 1896 soon after the birth of the cinema. Like the first photographs in colour, they were hand-painted. Films were shown at sixteen pictures per second and the first films, about fifty feet in length and lasting about fifty seconds, contained over 700 individual pictures. The colouring was done by girls, each of whom applied one colour only. Although the*

[7] D.B. Thomas, **The First Colour Motion Pictures**, (London: HMSO, 1969) p. 2

work involved in hand-painting a fifty foot length of film would seem prodigious, the cost of colouring in 1902 was only 35/- per fifty feet of film on top of the usual cost at that time of 21/- for the black and white print.[7]

As the figures quoted here suggest, hand-painting and hand-tinting were economically viable under conditions such as these. Relatively cheap as a colour print may have been though, it still cost 50 per cent more than a black and white one. Economics cannot have been the only factor involved. Clearly there were aesthetic and ideological motivations behind the production of colour prints right from the beginnings of film, at a time when the only means of producing those prints were, indeed, 'prodigous'.

The Pathécolor Printing Room.
*Courtesy Kodak Museum*

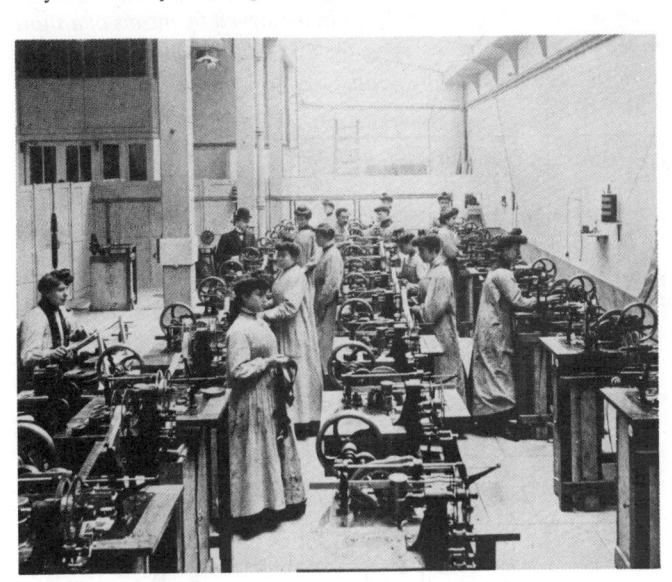

## Pathécolor and the Handschiegl Process

By the mid-1900s, the average length of films had increased. So had the number of cinemas and other exhibition venues, making for an increase too in the number of prints required for each film. Under these conditions hand-colouring as a widespread practice became impracticable, unprofitable and generally uneconomic.

Its place was taken by stencilling techniques, pioneered by the French company Pathé, as Pathécolor:

> The stencils (one for each colour) were made with machines which resembled pantographs. An enlarged image of one frame of the film was projected on to a ground-glass screen in front of the operator. She traced the outline of the areas required to be in one particular colour. Her stencil, as it touched the glass, brought together two cutting tools on either side of the film, cutting out the stencil image. The film was then advanced one frame and the operation repeated. After the stencil had been made for the whole length of the film, it was placed in contact with the film which was to be coloured, and the two films were run through a machine which applied colour through the holes in the stencil by means of a short endless band of velvet carrying the dye. The stencil-coloured films were finally retouched by hand.[8]

8. Thomas, **The First Colour Motion Pictures**, pp. 2–4

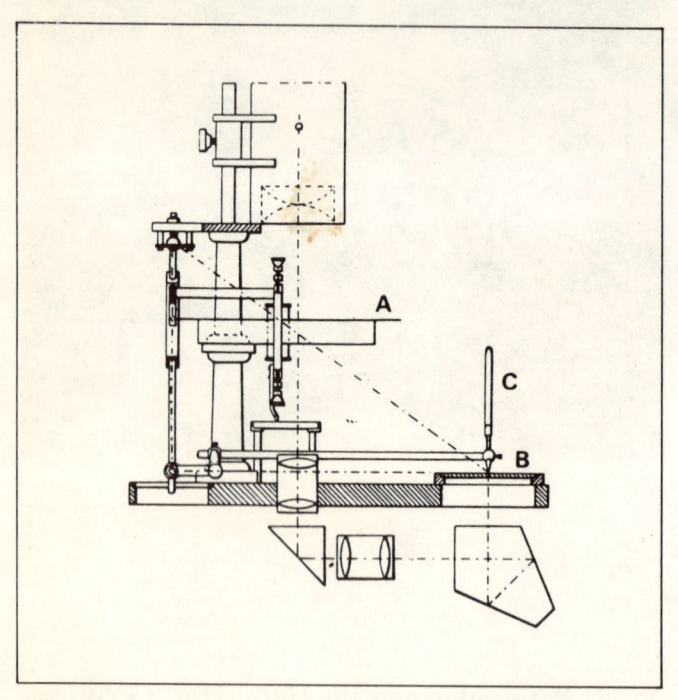

Diagram of stencil-making machine. A magnified image of one frame of a film A is projected on to ground glass at B. The operator traces an outline with the rod C. The depression of the rod closes an electrical circuit activating the cutting tools. From D.B. Thomas, **The First Colour Motion Pictures**, p. 3

By 1910 Pathé was employing some 400 workers entirely on hand and machine colouring at their factory in Vincennes, and the Pathécolor process itself was still being used in the early 1930s.

Compared to the process of hand-painting individual frames, the Pathécolor stencilling process was clearly a step

# Early examples of stencil colouring

From a series of epic Italian films on the life of Christ, c. 1909

From newsreel fashion sequences, c. 1912

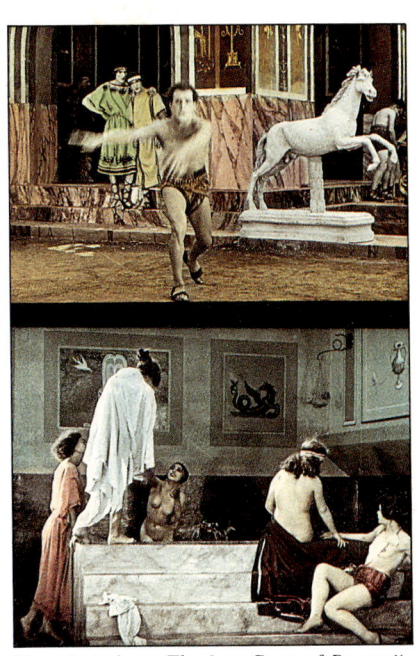

Two shots from *The Last Days of Pompeii* (Carmine Gallone/Amleto Palermi, 1926)

i

# Examples of tinting and toning

An arsonist at work, *c.* 1910. He enters a factory at night to set fire to it; as the flames flare up the shot is tinted red

*c.* 1920. The transition from night exterior to yellow-tinted lamplit interior has a similar effect

*c.* 1924. Chemical toning

*c.* 1924. The two techniques of tinting and toning combined to produce colour effects

# The Kinemacolor process

Black and white prints of *The Delhi Durbar* (1912)

A colour record of the above

# Technicolor

*Ben Hur* (Fred Niblo, 1925). One of the first films to be made using a two-colour subtractive process with a beam-splitting camera

Walt Disney's Silly Symphony *Flowers and Trees* (1931). © 1984 Walt Disney Productions

# Technicolor

*Becky Sharp* (Rouben Mamoulian, 1935). Courtesy RKO

*Henry V* (Laurence Olivier, 1944). Courtesy The Rank Organisation plc

# Technicolor

*Three Musketeers* (George Sidney, 1948). Courtesy MGM-UA

*Black Narcissus* (Michael Powell/Emeric Pressburger, 1947)

# Technicolor

*Across the Wide Missouri* (William Wellman, 1951). Courtesy MGM-UA

# Eastman Color

*Kismet* (Vincente Minnelli, 1955). Courtesy MGM-UA

towards the mechanisation of the production of colour prints, a step towards the mass production and automation of colour in film. The Handschiegl process was to some extent another, combining in the labour process aspects both of artisanal production and of automation and mechanical mass production. Max Handschiegl was an engraver in St Louis who adapted some of the principles of engraving in the production of colour prints:

> Finished productions were brought to Handschiegl; he would then etch, print, or hand block a 'register print' of the portions of the film selected for color treatment. The result of his work became the 'color plate', similar to the plates used in lithography. Examples of the Handschiegl process can be seen in sequences within D.W. Griffith's **Birth of a Nation** *(1915) and* **Intolerance** *(1916), Cecil B. DeMille's* **Joan the Woman** *(1917), Douglas Fairbanks'* **The Three Musketeers** *(1921), and* **When Knighthood was in Flower** *(1922) starring Marion Davies.*[9]

9. Fred E. Barsten, Glorious Technicolor (London: A.S. Barnes, 1980) p. 14

## Tinting and Toning

With film production, distribution and exhibition nationally and internationally becoming rapidly organised along conventional industrial lines, with rapid growth and the consequent increase in demand for more and more prints, the move towards the elimination of artisanal modes of production and the introduction of mechanisation and standardisation continued at all levels in the industry. These existing methods of applying colour to film became, in this context, not only time-consuming, but also increasingly expensive. As a consequence, the processes of 'tinting' and 'toning' were increasingly adopted in the production of colour prints.

Tinting involved the immersion of black-and-white film into any one of a number of standard dyes (trade names included Peachglow, Firelight, Sunshine, Azure, Nocturne, Inferno, Argent and so on). The dye was absorbed by the gelatin in the emulsion on the film base, thus giving each frame, segment, sequence or scene a uniform colour throughout. The common practice was to tint each scene according to mood and to the specifics of the setting and action: a fire scene would be tinted red, a night scene blue, a sunlit scene yellow and so on. Tinting was obviously dependent upon the production by the chemical companies of a standardised range of colour dyes, and it is a significant indication of the importance of tinting in film (and the widespread extent of its use) that a number of chemical companies (the National Aniline and Chemical Company, the White Tar Aniline Corporation and others) seemed to some extent to specialise in the production of dyes for the film industry.

Toning, unlike tinting, involves colouring only the black silver image on the film. Rather than producing an overall uniform colour, it colours only the half-tones and shadows, leaving the highlights translucent. The process works as follows:

> *The black and white photographic image consists of finely divided silver which can be converted into almost any insoluble silver salt. When the silver is converted into a coloured salt the process is known as "chemical toning" and the image is produced in the colour of the compound which replaces the original silver. Thus if we treat a black and white film with potassium ferrocyanide the silver is converted to blue-green ferrocyanide and we get a blue-green image. By choice of reagent it is possible to produce an image of yellow, magenta or almost any colour. The image, being translucent, presents a coloured image on the screen.*[10]

If, as has already been noted, tinting and toning were much used during the 1920s, 'when a film entirely in black-and-white was a relative rarity',[11] it may well be asked why the practice itself became a rarity after the coming of sound. One immediate and persuasive answer is a simple, technological one:

> with the introduction of sound the existing types of tinted [film] base became unusable. Unfortunately, the majority of dyes used in tinting absorbed the wavelengths of radiation to which the sound reproducer cells are most sensitive. The dyes reduced the response of the cell to such a great extent that high amplification of the photoelectric currents was required to obtain sufficient volume of sound. This high amplification increased the inherent cell noises and microphone disturbances in the amplifier so that the reproduced sound was of intolerably poor quality. For this reason, the use of tinted film was discontinued entirely in the production of positives carrying a photographic sound record.[12]

This, however, is not quite so complete and straightforward an answer as it may seem. Dyes, suitably modified, continued to be produced. In 1929 Eastman Kodak brought out their Sonochrome range, 'a spectrum of sixteen delicate atmospheric colors keyed to the mood of the screen . . . for silent or sound pictures'.[13] Moreover, the practice of tinting and toning continued, in selected instances, for many years, particularly in sepia-tinted western films. Among the more notable

10. Thomas, **The First Colour Motion Pictures**, p. 4
11. Roger Manvell (ed.), **The International Encyclopedia of Film** (London: Michael Joseph, 1972) p. 29

12. Ryan, **A History of Motion Picture Colour Technology**, pp. 16–17

13. L.A. Jones, 'Tinted Films for Sound Positives', **Transactions of the Society of Motion Picture Engineers,** May 1929, p. 199

*latterday achievements using these techniques were the sepia tones of Twentieth Century-Fox's* **The Rains Came** *(1939), United Artists'* **Of Mice and Men** *(1940). Metro-Goldwyn-Mayer's* **Ziegfeld Girl** *(1941) and* **Tortilla Flat** *(1942), the green-tinted storm sequences in David O. Selznick's* **Portrait of Jenny** *(1948), and the multiple tints in RKO's* **Mighty Joe Young** *(1949).*[14]

14. Basten, **Glorious Technicolor**, pp. 14–15

So the technical problems of using tinting and toning processes with optical sound were not, ultimately, insoluble. It seems much more likely that the demise of tinting and toning as the basis for the mass production of the bulk of colour films and colour sequences in films after the coming of sound was due rather to a combination of technical, aesthetic and ideological factors. With the coming of sound the whole aesthetic regime of cinema changed to an evident extent. Sound definitively marked a shift towards what was conceived as a kind of realism: sound was added to image, speech to the body, dialogue to the fiction, and so on. And this realism had a particular technological base, both in theory and in practice, that is synchronised, recorded sound. The use of tinting and toning within the aesthetic and ideological regime of late silent cinema was specific, and differed to some extent from the new canons of aesthetic realism established with the coming of sound. Tinting and toning were an integral part of what might be termed a symbolic or poetic or rhetorical realism, in which effects of gesture, lighting and colour were motivated as much by mood (itself motivated by theme or plot) as by narrative or diegetic logic. The usual practice was to colour a particular scene or sequence a uniform shade, tint or hue, in accordance with the mood of the scene or with its general temporal or spatial location. In tinting processes at least, literally everything in the image was given the same colour (whatever the colour of the clothes the actors were wearing and the objects with which they were surrounded). The strictly realistic demands of colour were thus strongly counter-balanced by symbolic, poetic or rhetorical demands which were clearly in accord with the technological possibilities. There was no real contradiction between the aesthetic and the technology. However, with the introduction of sound, a new aesthetic (or a new aesthetic orientation) made itself manifest *at the same time* as a set of real (but potentially and actually soluble) short-term technological problems. Ultimately the colour technology appropriate, so to speak, to the predominant aesthetic of sound cinema was found in 'natural' photographic colour systems (Technicolor's two-colour system was introduced and first widely used in the early 1930s, followed by its three-colour system). This general point is one to which I shall later return. In the meantime, though, we need to take a look at some of the photographic colour systems introduced and developed during the silent period, including those of early Technicolour.

## Early 'Additive' Processes

The first 'natural' colour processes for film were additive processes, derived from James Clerk Maxwell's experiments with still photographs and colour filters. The Lee and Turner process, for example, was invented towards the turn of the nineteenth century, and involved a camera shutter consisting of three opaque sectors alternating with red, green and blue colour filters. The film itself thus consisted of a recurring series of red, green and blue exposures. Since the film stock used at this time was orthochromatic, and thus more sensitive to blue-violet light than to red and green, the Lee and Turner patent pointed out that the opaque sectors of the shutter could be increased or decreased in order to produce the required balance of blue, green and red filter exposures. As tended to be the case with most additive processes, the mode of projection was a complicated one, requiring a modification both of the basic projection apparatus and/or of the speed with which the film was shown:

> Three consecutive frames of the film were projected on to the screen simultaneously by means of three projection lenses placed very close together. Each frame of the film was projected three times, first through the upper lens, then through the middle lens, and finally through the lower lens. The colour was provided by a synchronised rotating three-sectored shutter bearing concentric bands of colour filters . . . Suppose we consider a red frame (one which was photographed through a red filter). When it is projected through the upper lens the beam of light passes through the outer red filter of the shutter. It is then moved down to the middle lens and projected through the middle red filter of the shutter. Through the lower lens it is projected through the inner red filter of the shutter. The film, of course, moves intermittently and while it is moving the projection light is masked by the opaque portions of the filter disc. [See diagram opposite].[15]

15. Thomas, **The First Colour Motion Pictures**, p. 5

When Lee withdrew his backing in 1901, Turner approached Charles Urban, Managing Director of the British motion picture company, the Warwick Trading Company, which distributed films by Williamson, Meliès, Lumière, G.A. Smith and others. Turner died the following year, after designing what

Shutter of Lee and Turner projector. In this diagram the red portions of the filters are reproduced as dark grey, the green portions as medium grey and the blue portions as light grey. From D.B. Thomas. **The First Colour Motion Pictures,** p. 5

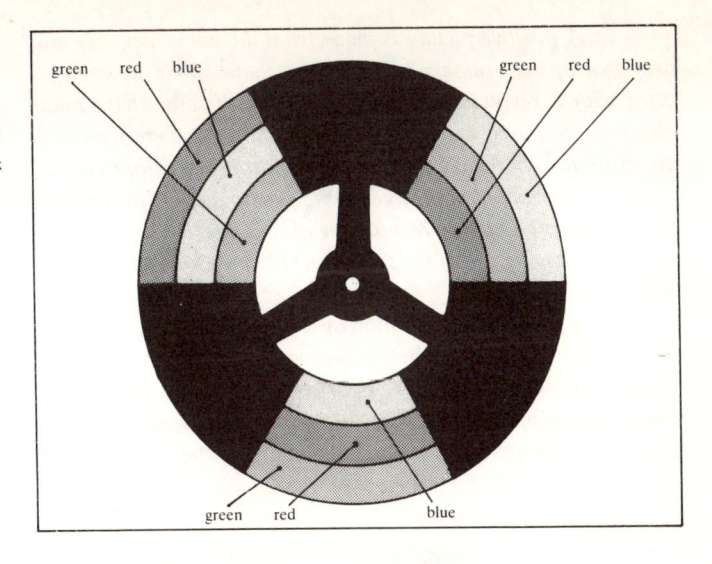

proved to be an unsuccessful three-colour projector. Urban acquired the patent rights to the Lee and Turner process and financed G.A. Smith to work on improving it. After attempts at producing a three-colour system which involved projection at three times normal speed (and thus excessive wear and tear on the film), Smith began work on a two-colour process which became the basis of the most successful of the early colour processes, Kinemacolor.

## Kinemacolor

Using just two colours, red and green instead of three, filming and projection speeds in Kinemacolor were reduced to 32 frames per second, thus reducing also the cost of the film and wear in the camera and projector. The patent, dated November 1906, describes the process as follows:

*An animated picture of a coloured scene is taken with a bioscope camera in the usual way, except that a revolving shutter is used fitted with properly adjusted red and green colour screens. A negative is thus obtained in which the reds and yellows are recorded in one picture, and the greens and yellows (with some blue) in the second, and so on alternately throughout the length of the bioscope film.*

*A positive picture is made from the above negative and projected by the ordinary projecting machine which, however, is fitted with a revolving shutter furnished with somewhat similar glasses to the above, and so contrived that the red and green pictures are projected alternately through their appropriate colour glasses.*

*If the speed of projection is approximately 30 pictures per second, the two colour records blend and present to the eye a satisfactory rendering of the subject in colours which appear to be natural.*[16]

16. Quoted in Thomas, **The First Colour Motion Pictures**, p. 14

The first demonstration of Kinemacolor took place on 1 May 1908 in London, the first public demonstration at the Palace Theatre of Varieties on 26 February 1909. The programme included typical actuality pieces like **Waves and Spray** as well as scenes and sequences designed to highlight the properties of

Kinemacolor projector. *Courtesy Science Museum*

122

colour cinematography in the representation of nature and in the production of spectacle: **Sweet Flowers, Carnival Scenes at Nice and Cannes, Children's Battle of Flowers, Nice** and **Church Parade of the 7th and 16th Lancers.**

In March 1909, Urban formed the Natural Color Kinematograph Company to handle the production and distribution of Kinemacolor films. The Kinemacolor projector, modified by Henry Joly in 1910, was heavier than conventional projection machines in order to reduce the vibration produced by running at double speed. The Kinemacolor camera was a conventional camera fitted with a synchronised filter shutter. Kinemacolor films were shown initially only at the Palace Theatre in London, and then in Nottingham and Blackpool. Then in 1911, Urban began showing complete programmes of Kinemacolor films at the Scala near Tottenham Court Road in London. The first programmes comprised news and actuality films such as the Coronation and the Investiture, though dramas and comedies were in production at Hove during the summer months and at Nice during the winter. Instead of changing the programme once or twice a week, as was conventional exhibition practice at that time, programmes ran for several months. The following year, Urban's greatest success, a film of the Delhi Durbar, which ran for two and a half hours, was shown in England, Ireland, Scotland and Wales and grossed over £150,000 in fifteen months. This proved to be the peak of Kinemacolor's popularity. Dramas like **Mephisto, Oedipus Rex** and **The World The Flesh and The Devil** were less successful.

Kinemacolor was tried in France, Italy, Canada, Holland, the United States and elsewhere without a great deal of success. Following a patent judgement against Kinemacolor in 1915, and Urban's departure to the United States to publicise the British war effort, Kinemacolor declined until after 1916 it became to all intents and purposes defunct.

## Chronochrome and Prizmacolor

Kinemacolor was by no means the only colour process in existence before or during the period of the development of Technicolor (from 1915 onwards). There were processes such as Kinchrome, Kromoscope, Zoechrome, Kelleycolor, Colorcraft and others, some of which never went beyond the experimental stage, others of which were used once or twice, usually only in demonstration form. None were in existence for more than a few years, and few were employed in commercial production and exhibition. Kinemacolor was in this respect far and away the most successful of the colour processes in existence at this time. Before going on to look at some of the reasons for its ultimate demise, it is worth looking in a little more detail at two of the other, and far less successful, colour processes developed during the 1910s, Chronochrome and Prizmacolor, since some of the conditions for the commercial failure of all the colour processes developed at that time, including Kinemacolor, can be highlighted through these other examples. One can then begin also to identify some of the reasons for the ultimate, though initially intermittent, success of Technicolor.

Chronochrome was a three-colour process developed by Gaumont during the period 1912–13. It was demonstrated in France in November 1912 and in England in January 1913, though it never reached the stage of regular public exhibition. The system worked as follows:

> Chronochrome negatives were obtained in a camera equipped with three lenses, placed one above the other, each fitted with a glass filter. The negative produced consisted of red, green and blue colour records, each colour record recurring every third frame. Three images, one on the red record, one on the green record and the third the blue record, were simultaneously projected through three lenses fitted with filters to produce a natural colour picture on the screen . . . During projection the projection lenses and filters had to be carefully aligned to produce the screen image as accurately in register as possible. This was effected by moving the top and bottom lenses in three directions by an alignment mechanism, the middle lens being fixed.[17]

17. Quoted in Thomas, **The First Colour Motion Pictures**, p. 36

The height of the standard frame of 35 mm film was reduced in order to reduce the length of film required to shoot a sequence and in order to lessen the strain placed on the film. Even so, the required projection speed was 48 frames per second.

Attempts to improve the Kinemacolor process were made by William van Doren Kelly of Prizma Incorporated in America, the principle behind the improvements being the attempt to produce the blue-green and red-orange photographic records simultaneously rather than successively. He produced a camera with two lenses, one above the other. However, the images formed by the lenses were produced from slightly different points of view, and so could not be identically matched in projection. The process was first demonstrated in New York on 8 February 1917.

Kelly next went on to try and develop a subtractive colour system, using dyes rather than filters:

> His negatives were produced in a Kinemacolor type of camera and had the red and green records on alternate frames along the film. For printing positives he used double coated film stock, film which has a sensitive emulsion coating on both back and front of the film base. The film base of such a film is made opaque to printing light by means of an appropriate dye so that when one side of the film is exposed to printing light the light does not penetrate through the base to affect the emulsion on the reverse side. During processing this dye is dissolved out to leave the transparent base between the two emulsions. The orange-red record of the Prizma two-colour film was printed on one side of the double coated film, the blue-green record on the other side. If we take the case of the 'red' images, after one 'red' image has been printed, the positive is moved along one frame while the negative, which has red records alternately along the film, is moved along two frames. When the 'green' images have been printed on the other side of the film we now have the two silver images one on each side of the film in register . . .[18]

18. Quoted in Thomas, **The First Colour Motion Pictures**, p. 38

Having printed the two colour records, the next step was to convert the black silver images into the appropriate colours. One method was to use chemical toning agents. Another was to harden the gelatin in which the image was registered in proportion to the amount of silver. The hardened portions of gelatin left once the silver is dissolved away could be dyed the appropriate colour. A feature film called **The Glorious Adventure** was shot in the Prizma subtractive process in England in 1921. It was not an immediate success, however, probably due in large part to the cost. Prints of **The Glorious Adventure** cost 25 cents per foot, six times the price of conventional black and white film.

## The Failure of the Early Additive Systems

The first Prizma process and Gaumont's Chronochrone shared with Kinemacolor the fundamental technical property of being additive rather than subtractive. To the extent that they shared this property they shared also a set of basic technical problems and drawbacks which, in the context of the practices of the film industry as they were developing at that time, contributed in varying degrees to their failure. Additive proceses all suffered from registration problems in projection. With Prizma, the double lens system produced parallax problems, since the two differently coloured images were taken from different viewpoints through different lenses. Chronochrome required a complex registration device in projection in order to align the three projection lenses. According to Ernest Coustet, the projectionist had in fact to be connected by telephone to someone sitting close to the screen, who would tell him when the lenses needed realignment.[19] Kinemacolor too had its problems in this respect:

*A period of time of about 1/30th of a second elapsed between the 'red' exposure and the 'green' exposure in the camera. During this time interval some movement of the subject took place with the result that the two consecutive exposures produced frames which were not identical and so perfect registration or superimposition on the screen was impossible. Coloured fringes were seen around moving objects.*[20]

In addition to registration difficulties, all systems involving the use of filters were hampered by the need for particularly good lighting conditions, both in filming and in projection, particularly when, as in the case of Kinemacolor and Chronochrome, films were taken at near twice the speed of black and white film, thus reducing exposure time. At this time film studios were using artificial lighting more and more to supplement or replace natural light. One of the new and most commonly used lights, the Cooper-Hewitt mercury vapour lamp, because it was weak in red and green and strong in blue and violet light, was suitable for black and white film but useless for colour.

These are all technical difficulties, but they spill over and interconnect with factors to do as much with economics and the practices of the film industry at that time as with technology *per se*. For instance, the fact that additive systems required modifications to existing projection equipment was not in itself a problem. The problem was rather that the wholesale adoption of such modifications would have required money in a branch of the industry which has historically always been notoriously conservative (witness subsequent problems, difficulties and failures with regard to the introduction of widescreen and 3-D systems and to substantial improvements in sound available on magnetic rather than optical sound tracks). If colour were to be adopted on a large scale the systems that stood the best chance would be systems requiring little or no modification to existing projection equip-

19. Ernest Coustet, **Le Cinéma** (Paris: Librairie Hachette, 1921) p. 173

20. Thomas **The First Colour Motion Pictures**, p. 31

ment. The success that Kinemacolor enjoyed for a time was particular; it was not the kind of success resulting in the wholesale adoption of the process by the film industry as such. Rather, as with the much later Cinerama process, it involved long runs of a limited number of films and programmes at a limited and particular number of cinemas. This is emphasised all the more by the types of film made in Kinemacolor and by the types of film that proved especially popular: news, actuality, and non-fiction in general at a time when fiction (dramas and comedies) tended overwhelmingly to dominate mainstream production.

A further factor, or set of related factors, already mentioned a number of times in passing, concerned the cost of additive colour film. And this in a number of very direct ways. Because Kinemacolor and Chronochrome involved shooting at speeds much higher than those involved in conventional black and white films, the cost of raw stock was that much more expensive. And because the speed both of filming and of projection was faster, so film stock and prints were worn out that much quicker and needed more rapid replacement. The only factor that could have outweighed these cost factors would have been popularity and hence, profit. It would seem, however, that such demand as there was for colour was met quite adequately, and more cheaply and less laboriously, by tinting and toning.

In the particular case of Kinemacolor, finally, one or two other specific factors seem to have been involved. Urban was working from Britain. In order to achieve expanding and more lasting success he needed to penetrate American and European markets. Having bought the rights to the Kinemacolor patent, he followed a restrictive policy of expansion, granting licences to showmen in a specific area which enabled that showman to use the projector and film Urban supplied him. His policy and practice internationally was similar. He generally sought to sell the patent rights to a particular individual or enterprise. In operating in this way he was working in a similar fashion to many of the early patent holders on film and film equipment. All were ultimately to fail after a limited period of success because patent rights were ignored or challenged, because at a time of rapid expansion a more longlastingly successful strategy would have been to seek to expand rather than restrict the use of a particular invention and because, eventually, law courts were historically to decide against patent holders either in conventional patent disputes (as happened to Urban) or in anti-monopoly proceedings (as happened to the patents trust in America). In Urban's case, lack of penetration of foreign markets tended to be due to his restrictive policies. Foreign patent holders were left on their own as it were, and were thus vulnerable to pressures from entrenched, successful and wealthy companies producing conventional black and white films. In the case of America, ironically, a crucial market at this time owing to its rapid expansion during the First World War, Urban was held in check by the restrictive practices of the Motion Picture Patents Company:

*He came to the United States in 1912 and offered the Kinemacolor process to the United States Patents Company. After a successful test showing, they made him a good offer. The offer, however, was intended to suppress his invention and keep him out of the colour field.*[21]

21. James L. Limbacher, **Four Aspects of the Film**, p. 16

The Patents Company was eventually to remove its bars, but by then Kinemacolor itself was only to last for a few more years.

# 8:
## Technicolor

## The Beginnings of Technicolor

The very first Technicolor colour process was also an additive one, sharing, with Kinemacolor, Chronochrome and the rest similar technical features and, therefore, similar technical and potential commercial problems. Technicolor's success stemmed ultimately from having developed a practical subtractive process (or set of processes) which it constantly refined and developed, thus eliminating the need for special projection equipment and for separate research and development programmes on the part of the major studios and production companies. In addition, Technicolor was to concentrate from the 1930s on on shooting colour films and colour sequences for separate production companies rather than on producing its own films, as Kinemacolor did.

Technicolor was formed as a corporation in 1915 on the basis of $10,000 advanced by a Boston corporation lawyer to its founders, Herbert Kalmus, Daniel Comstock and Barton Prescott. Kalmus had a Bachelor of Science degree from the Massachusettes Institute of Technology. Daniel Comstock taught at the Institute and three of his students, Leonard Troland, Joseph Ball and Eastman Weaver were to provide much technical and scientific help. Technicolor's first process, a two-color additive system, was developed in 1916 and used to shoot its first feature, **The Gulf Between,** the following year. Like all Technicolor's systems, this one involved obtaining two simultaneous colour records in filming by means of a prism in the camera. Part of the light entering the camera lens was reflected through a red filter to give a red record. The rest was reflected through a green filter to give a green record. The prism device was to evolve in the early 1920s into Technicolor's beam-splitting camera, which was to feature in its subsequent subtractive systems (see diagram below).

Technicolor beam-splitter camera

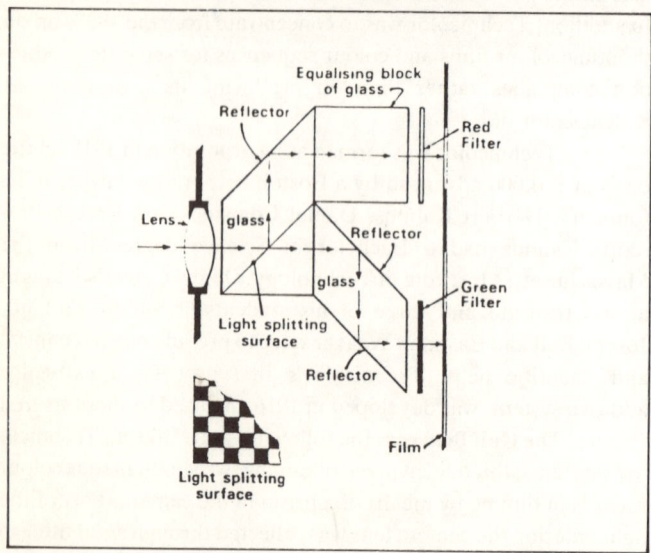

Sectional diagram of an early Technicolor camera, c. 1920. From D.B. Thomas, **The First Colour Motion Pictures**, p. 39

As with other additive systems, most of the problems came at the projection stage. Technicolor's registration device proved so delicate and difficult to operate that, according to Herbert Kalmus' own account, a decision was made after only a few showings of **The Gulf Between** to abandon additive systems and to explore the possibilities of developing a subtractive one:

> *I decided that such special attachments on the projector required an operator who was a cross between a college professor and an acrobat... Technicolor then and there abandoned 'additive' processes and special attachments on the projector.*[1]

1. Quoted in Basten, Glorious Technicolor, p. 28

## Technicolor's First Subtractive Processes

Work on Technicolor's second process, its first subtractive process, began in 1919. Work on the beam-splitting camera began a year earlier. The system was eventually developed in 1922, progress having been slowed down by lack of funds. Financial support was eventually obtained from lawyers, advertising executives and people like John McHugh of the Chase National Bank. Marcus Loew, and Nicholas and Joseph Schenck, prominent figures in the American film industry, were also interested, though they provided no direct financial support. The new system involved the use of the beam-splitting camera during filming. From the two separate negatives, two dyed positive 'relief' images were produced, as Kalmus later explained:

> *By a relief image I mean that instead of having silver deposits constituting the image of the picture as printed from the negative, hills and valleys are etched in the gelatin giving a relief image corresponding with the image of the picture. Two such relief images, one each for the red and green components, were welded together back to back in register. Then the two sides, one after the other, were floated over baths of the respective dyes and dried. Thus, we made a double-coated relief image in dyes.*[2]

2. Quoted Basten, Glorious Technicolor, p. 29

The system having been developed, Technocolor was offered facilities, a director (Chester Franklin) and a star (Anna May Wong) by Loew's in order to shoot a feature, **The Toll of the Sea**. The film was distributed by Metro and received its première at the Rialto Theatre in New York in November 1922. The film grossed some $250,000 of which Technicolor received $165,000.

There were problems, however. Technicolor had no adequate means of providing rush prints, and had to charge 20 cents per foot for release prints. This problem was alleviated to some extent by opening a small laboratory and photographic unit in Hollywood. (This was important. According to Hal Hall and William Stull, one of the major reasons for the ultimate failure of Prizma's subtractive system was the fact that the company remained based in Jersey City: 'Had it joined the rest of the industry in its Westward trek, there is no doubt that it would be with us today'.)[3] There were further difficulties over the technique of cementing the two coloured positives together. The film tended to 'cup' as it went through the projector, something which was a problem not only in itself, so to speak, but also inasmuch as it placed a further strain on Technicolor's print service when prints needed replacement and repair. There were problems too at the production stage. High intensity lighting was required, which caused difficulties for the actors.

3. Hal Hall and William Stull, 'Motion Pictures in Natural Colours', **Cinematographic Annual,** 1930, vol. 1, p. 278

The process was technically and aesthetically successful enough to be used further while Technicolor worked on improving its system. **Wanderer of the Wasteland** was shot for Famous Players-Lasky, and then several dream-sequences were shot in the studio for Sam Goldwyn's **Cytherea.** The following year, 1925, the Technicolor process was used to shoot Douglas' Fairbanks **The Black Pirate.**

The use of cemented positives, meanwhile, had proved particularly intractable, and in 1928, Technicolor announced the development of its second two-colour subtractive process. This process involved the use of a printing technique known as imbibition, eliminating the need for two separate, cemented positive prints. With the imbibition process, what is known as a matrix is produced, from which the final print is made. The matrix is a positive bearing a relief image. One matrix is made for each of the two colours in the process and appropriately dyed. Both matrices are then used to transfer the dye images in registration to the final print film. Although requiring very accurate registration, the process transfers the problem of registration as a whole from the sphere of exhibition to the sphere of production, while obviating the need for cementing two separate prints together. Prints could be mass produced from the matrices, and required no special projection conditions whatsoever.

The introduction of Technicolor's second subtractive process coincided with the introduction of optical sound. Two particular factors related to the coming of sound were instrumental in producing a real, though shortlived boom in the use of the new process. Unlike the tinting and toning processes then in use, the imbibition process did not affect the sound track. And unlike not only the first Technicolor subtractive process, but also Kodak's Sonochrome, a non-photographic tinted positive film developed in 1929 for use with sound, the new Technicolor process enabled the production of relatively durable prints, comparable to black-and-white ones. The second factor involved in the boom was the cycle of musicals produced in the late 1920s and early 1930s. Given the aesthetic association that existed at that time (and indeed, with some variation, up until the 1960s) between colour, fantasy and spectacle, it is no accident that the new system was used either to shoot particular sequences in the musicals, such as production numbers, or else to shoot the whole film. Films like **Gold Diggers of Broadway** (1929), **On With The Show** (1929), **Song of the West** (1930) and **The Melody Man** (1930) were shot wholly in the new Technicolor process, while sequences were shot for **Broadway Melody** (1929), **The Desert Song** (1929), **Rio Rita** (1929), **Putting on the Ritz** (1930), **No, No Nanette** (1930) and many others.

The boom lasted only for a couple of years, however. With the comparatively enormous and sudden demand put on Technicolor's process and facilities for filming and for the production of release prints, quality began to decline. The Depression, meanwhile, was causing dwindling attendance and box-office figures. Producers were more and more reluctant to pay for the use of the process once it became clear that colour of itself could not maintain or attract bigger audiences and profits.

Technicolor, however, were still working on modifications and improvements to their colour systems, and in 1932, when the boom in musicals and in colour was firmly at an end, they announced the development of the three-colour subtractive process that was to form the basis of their virtual monopoly in the colour field up until the appearance of Eastmancolor in the early 1950s.

## The First Three-colour Subtractive System

Introducing a third primary colour, blue, into its subtractive colour technology, and being thus theoretically capable of incorporating the visible spectrum much more widely and accurately into its aesthetic and technical ambit, the new system worked as follows:

*The Technicolor three-strip camera exposed three sepa-*

rate black-and-white negatives simultaneously through a single lens. Immediately behind this lens was a beam-splitter made by two prisms of optical glass which were gold coated (later silver flecked) to produce a slight mirrored effect. The purpose of the beam-splitter was to reflect part of the light to an aperture to the left. The remaining light passed directly through to a normally positioned aperture.

The ray of light that passed directly through the prism reached a green filter that allowed only green light (or a green image) to reach the negative behind it. The reflected beam of light was directed to a standard bi-pack containing two negatives. The front film carried a red-orange dye which absorbed the blue light and filtered out the red rays. These rays passed through to register on the rear film of the pair.[4] [see diagram below]

4. Basten, **Glorious Technicolor**, pp. 199–201

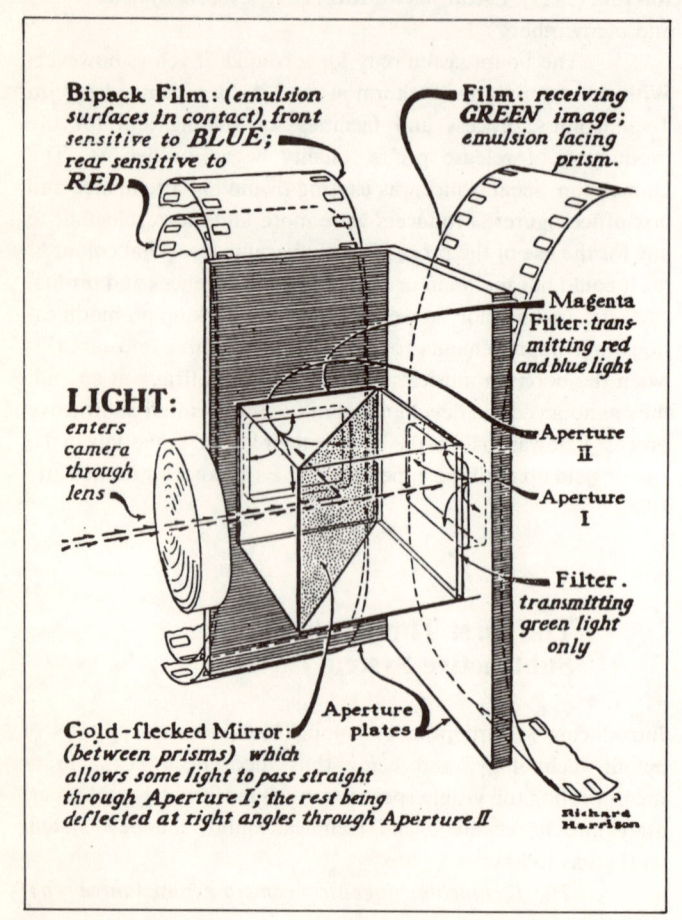

Diagram of three-colour subtractive system. From Basten, **Glorious Technicolor**, p. 200

The next step was to produce negatives from the exposed film and then to produce matrices from the negatives. As in the two-colour matrix process, the matrices were dyed and then used to produce positive prints:

> While the matrices were being made, a special dye-receptive blank film was prepared. If the customer wanted prints with optical sound tracks, the silver sound record was incorporated in the blank film at this stage. If the customer's prints were to carry magnetic sound tracks, the silver sound record was omitted and the magnetic tracks were applied after the dye transfer. Each matrix was dyed on a dye transfer machine with its complementary, or opposite, colour. The red matrix was brought into contact with a blue-green dye called cyan (blue-green being complementary to red). The green matrix was dyed with a magenta dye (complementary to green) and the blue matrix was dyed with a yellow dye (complementary to blue) . . .
>
> When each of the three matrices had been processed through the dye transfer machine, the once blank film contained all the colors necessary for excellent reproduction of the color sccene and was ready for delivery to exhibitors for projection. Where yellow dye was present, blue light was subtracted from the projector's white light source. Similarly, red was subtracted where cyan was present and green where magenta occurred. Absence of all dyes resulted in white light on the screen. The presence of all dyes in sufficient quantities created an absence of light, or a black image.[5]

5. Basten, **Glorious Technicolor**, pp. 202–3

Technicolor had completed the production of its first three-colour camera in May 1932. However, a number of factors militated against its widespread use, and contributed towards determining the channels for its use over the next few years. The new process was expensive. The cameras alone cost some $30,000 to build. Prints were expensive. And for producers there were extra costs involved in lighting, costuming, and scenery. The new process emerged at the end of the period of popularity of the two-colour process, whose lack of sustained success and impact on attendance and box-office figures during a period of depression tended to make major producers both sceptical and cautious. This scepticism and caution tended to be shared by those writing about colour technology at this time. Adrian Bernard Klein, for instance, writing in 1936, argues that the industry is unlikely to see a rapid move toward the adoption of Technicolor's system:

> Not the least cogent reason for thinking this is the cost of negative and positive film stock for colour as compared to black-and-white. Unless remarkable economies can be effected on

some other important items of the cost of making a film, it is very difficult to see how the extra cost of negative and positive is going to be borne by producers; especially as it is universally admitted that it is going to be impossible to make more out of a film just because it happens to be in colour, for the very simple reason that the public won't pay more to see it.[6]

In consequence, Technicolor had difficulties in finding a producer willing to use its new process. Rather than becoming involved directly in production itself, it instead offered the process to two small independent producers, Walt Disney and Pioneer Films (Merian C. Cooper and John Whitney), both of whom, as Gorham Kindem has noted, were either previously or subsequently involved in other technological innovations.[7]

It was Disney who first used the process in his 'Silly Symphonies' cartoon series. The first, **Flowers and Trees**, and the subsequent **The Three Little Pigs** were enormously successful. Both won Oscars, and **The Three Little Pigs** grossed something approaching a quarter of a million dollars. Disney was offered a three-year contract for the exclusive use of three-colour Technicolor in the cartoon field, but, partly due to pressure from other major producers, this was subsequently reduced to one year. By 1934, Fox, MGM and Goldwyn were using three-colour sequences in films like **The Cat and the Fiddle, Kid Millions** and **The House of Rothschild.**

Pioneer produced the first three-colour live action film, **La Cucaracha**, in 1934. Encouraged by the success of **La Cucaracha**, Pioneer went on the following year to make the first three-colour feature, **Becky Sharp**, which proved, however, to be a commercial failure. Cooper and Whitney then went on to join with David O. Selznick to establish Selznick International, which took over the contract with Technicolor. Selznick went on to produce three very successful colour features in successive years in the late 1930s, **A Star is Born** (1937), **The Adventures of Tom Sawyer** (1938) and **Gone With The Wind** (1939), the latter helped by the introduction of refinements by Technicolor yielding superior colour rendition, less grain, sharper definition and greater depth of focus and requiring much lower lighting levels.

6. Adrian Bernard Klein, **Colour Cinematography** (London: Chapman & Hall, 1936) pp. 302–3

7. Gorham A. Kindem, 'Hollywood's Conversion to Color: The Technological, Economic and Aesthetic Factors', **Journal of the University Film Association** vol. XXXI, no. 2 (Spring 1979) p. 33

## Technicolor in the 1940s and 1950s

The success of these films, and the availability of the new, improved three-colour system led to a greater use of the three-colour system during the 1940s but a number of factors still continued to limit the production of colour features. Kindem lists some of them as follows:

*1) Technicolor's virtual monopoly over three-color services for feature films, 2) the high cost of color, and 3) limited markets for color.*[8]

Although, as Kindem suggests, there is evidence that Technicolor did not intentionally limit its colour facilities in order to maximise its profits, it was nevertheless the case that Technicolor's virtual monopoly over three-colour processes, combined with its policy of control over the use of the process, substantially limited the supply and availability of colour during the 1940s. From a rough average of just under 20 films per year in the early 1940s to a figure of 46 in 1949, the number of Technicolor films certainly increased, but would seem to have remained below the level of demand, as is evidenced by the anti-trust suits initiated against both Technicolor and Eastman Kodak in the mid-1940s. Such suits were stimulated by Technicolor's policy of total secrecy and security as regards its technical and scientific research and by its insistence on having an adviser or advisory team present during production. Its security measures became increasingly rigid:

*With competitors on the scene, the by-words were 'top security'. Very few people were privy to the know-how and workings within the various departments, or to the methods and procedures that were discovered (and constantly being improved) solely by trial and error. Almost no one was allowed to roam at will, even insiders. It was impossible to gain admittance to the processing lab, for example, without a pass or the personal accompaniment of top-level management. Those employees who worked on an operational level were compartmentalized and stayed exclusively within the boundaries of their specialities. Rarely was anyone transferred to another department or division and only a small number had an overall view of the workings of the company.*[9]

As Lewis Jacobs, writing in 1939, points out, the situation with Technicolor and its facilities was similar to the situation pertaining 'in the early days when attempts were made to keep the movie projector in the hands of the few.'[10] Technicolor equipment could not be bought, it could only be rented from Technicolor itself. Jacobs goes on to quote an article written for *The American Cinematographer* complaining about secrecy surrounding Technicolor's processes:

*If the color enthusiasts would turn over their processes intact to practical studio men, they might iron out the kinks from a practical angle and develop color's commercial application . . . Reports mainly have it that current color processes have all too*

---

8. Kindem, 'Hollywood's Conversion to Color', p. 33

9. Basten, **Glorious Technicolor**, pp. 91–3

10. Lewis Jacobs, **The Rise of the American Film** (New York: Harcourt Brace, 1939) p. 447

*definite limitations in reproduction capability under actual production conditions, that too little now is known about the play of light on colors, that cameras need design improvement and a wider range of performance, that processing is done behind barred doors, that costs are needlessly high, that the whole subject is smothered in uncalled-for pseudo-theory and technicalities and that young blades from science academies are not necessarily picture producers.*[11]

Such a quote is evidence not only of the frustration over the secrecy and control that Technicolor pursued, but also, in its call for work on colour from elsewhere to be handed over to studio technicians, of a wish on the part of producers to have access to and control over an increasingly popular and potentially profitable aspect of film technology.

Control was exercised not only at the level of the laboratory, but also at the level of production, through Technicolor's colour consultancy service:

*Starting in the mid-1920s, Technicolor had made available a color consulting service to work with the studios and designers prior to and during film production. Now that service was not only available but required — and expanded to include the upgrading of virtually every facet involved in color photography. A contract with Technicolor was a package that included not only the rental of the three-color camera but a Technicolor cameraman who worked as an advisor to the studio's cinematographer; advice given to art directors, set directors and designers, wardrobe and property departments; use of make-up and assistance to the studio make-up departments; the requirements of special lighting equipment; and laboratory processing up to and including the final release print.*[12]

This service, in addition to helping maintain Technicolor's monopoly, its control not only of colour technology as such, but also of colour aesthetics, contributed also to the costs of using colour. It was estimated that in 1935, colour added some 30 per cent to the production costs of a feature; in 1949, some 10 per cent.[13] In addition, during the 1940s, the differential costs between distributing colour and black-and-white feature films increased:

*The cost of Technicolor release prints increased from about 5 ¢/ft in 1940 to about 7 ¢/ft in 1949, while the cost of black-and-white prints remained about the same, almost 3 c/ft. In short, in terms of both production and distribution, it was obviously much less expensive to use black-and-white for a feature film than color, and hence, the cost differential between color and*

11. Quoted in Jacobs, **The Rise of the American Film**, pp. 447–8

12. Basten, **Glorious Technicolor**, p. 66

13. Kindem, 'Hollywood's Conversion to Color', p. 34

*black-and-white limited color feature film diffusion during the 1940s.*[14]

Finally, as Kindem has elaborated, there was still some uncertainty as to the market value of colour (as opposed to black and white) through the 1940s and into the 1950s. Colour was still overwhelmingly associated, aesthetically, with spectacle and fantasy. In consequence, colour continued to be regularly used in genres like the musical, the western and the adventure film, as well as in Disney's feature cartoons. Colour was used, through the 1940s and into the 1950s, in films like **Pinocchio, The Return of Frank James, The Thief of Baghdad, Billy the Kid, Dumbo, Western Union, Arabian Nights, Jungle Book, Broadway Rhythm, Buffalo Bill, Kismet, Meet Me In St Louis, Anchors Away, State Fair, The Bandit of Sherwood Forest, Ziegfeld Follies, Sinbad the Sailor, The Pirate, She Wore a Yellow Ribbon** and **The Three Musketeers.** Outside these genres, however, the aesthetic and market values of colour were less certain, less predictable and less profitable. Kindem finds that:

*The markets for color were not significantly greater for color features than for black-and-white features in the 1940s and 1950s. Of the top grossing films for each year from 1940 to 1949, 5½ were in black-and-white and 4½ were in Technicolor. In 1948* **Variety** *estimated that color added about 25% to a feature film's earning power.*[15]

However, Kindem argues, additional production costs for colour might come to around $10,000 on an average film costing about $1 million, and to this had to be added as much again for the increased cost of distribution prints. Kindem finds that 50 per cent of all features had receipts of $1 million or more; thus on an average film in colour the additional 20 per cent costs would be barely covered by the additional 25 per cent revenue. He therefore concludes that doubts about the commercial value of colour placed limits on colour feature film diffusion.

The period between the mid to late 1940s and the early to mid 1950s was one which saw a number of important developments, shifts and changes in the field of commercial colour feature film production. In 1947, the United States Department of Justice filed an anti-trust suit against Technicolor, charging restraint of trade; in 1949 Eastman Kodak introduced a single strip colour negative and printing film stock which opened the field to a number of new commercial colour processes; television began to exert enormous (and complex) pressures upon the film industry, shifting, among other things, the value of colour in film; and, partly as a response to this pressure, the industry introduced a number of technical and aesthetic innovations (notably widescreen) which required certain modifications to existing colour processes. Technicolour survived all these changes. Indeed, it retained a hegemonic position. But that position was based on different factors from the one it occupied in the 1930s and 1940s. Before going on to discuss these changes and developments in a little more detail, it is therefore probably worth saying something about the foundations of its early success at this point.

## The Contexts of Technicolor's Success

Technicolor's early success, its domination of the colour field in commercial film production during the 1930s and 1940s, was clearly due to the superiority of its colour technology and its colour processes, especially after the introduction of three-colour Technicolor in the early 1930s. That superiority gave it a clear lead in the market, enabling it to build up the position of near monopoly which eventually led to the anti-trust suit. But Technicolor's monopolistic position resulted not just from the colour processes themselves, but also from the practices in which Technicolor as a company engaged and from the consequent position it established *vis-à-vis* production, and, hence, Hollywood's major studios.

Technicolor, historically, was an off-shoot of Kalmus, Comstock and Westcott, an engineering firm engaging in technical research and offering technical consultation and advice. Its personnel were highly-trained science graduates, the firm and the personnel having strong links with the Massachusetts Institute of Technology. There was hence a sound scientific, technical and engineering base for the subsequent development of its colour processes and equipment. Compared to Eastman Kodak, Technicolor was a small company. Its success lay in taking financial risks and in investing heavily in research and development. Gorham Kindem compares this aspect of the two companies:

*Technicolor's major inventions involved substantial economic risk. Technicolor continued to invest heavily in research and development despite the fact that between 1923 and 1935 Technicolor, Inc., accumulated a net loss of $2 million. In 1931, Technicolor invested over $180,000 in research and development. Despite the fact that Technicolor possessed a virtual monopoly on three-color* *for feature films throughout the 1930s, it didn't actually profit after taxes until 1939.*

*Eastman Kodak, on the other hand, invested over $15 million in color photographic research between 1921 and 1948, but it also had net sales of $435 million compared to Technicolor's $20 million in 1948. In 1948, Eastman Kodak also secured its major patents upon colored couplers* [substances in the film emulsion or developing solution which form colour dyes during photochemical processing of the exposed film] *for Eastmancolor, while it invested $3 million in color research. Obviously, Eastman Kodak never undertook financial risks proportionately equal to Technicolor's in its quest to secure a virtual monopoly over film color through patent protection of its major inventions.*[16]

16. Kindem, 'Hollywood's Conversion to Color', pp. 31–2

Having established itself, Technicolor protected its position in two ways. First, it developed a policy of strict secrecy, leading to the kind of complex intra- and inter-departmental security described already. Secondly, it refused to challenge the studios in the sphere of production. It did produce films, early on, but much preferred to contract its facilities, expertise, equipment and advice to those already engaged and established in production. Technical innovation thus took place outside the studios proper (a feature colour had in common with sound), and it was precisely this division between production and technical innovation and servicing which enabled Technicolor, having demonstrated its technical superiority, to maintain and protect its position. And because there was no competition between the studios and producers on the one hand and Technicolor on the other, Technicolor's position was even further secured. The studios and producers needed Technicolor, just as Technicolor needed them. In this respect, the development of colour was different from the development of sound, as Lewis Jacobs has pointed out:

*The conditions affecting the progress of color are different. Most of the companies have a financial stake in Technicolor, so that there is little fear of competition to hurry Technicolor's development. Moreover, since these companies do not wish to relinquish the patent rights to the Technicolor process as Warner and Fox had to give up their rights to the electrical companies, and since they would dislike being faced by a competing color process, all scientific research in color is done in complete secrecy. There is little co-operation among laboratory workers; what knowledge there is about color is held by a few. As in the early days when attempts were made to keep the movie projector in the hands of the few, today Technicolor equipment cannot be bought; it can only be* rented with operator and crew. Negatives are processed behind the guarded doors of the Technicolor laboratory by Technicolor technicians.[17]

However, as was pointed out earlier, this secrecy eventually became a source of irritation and conflict, especially when Technicolor began to prove its financial worth, and especially among the smaller production companies who could either ill afford Technicolor's process or who, if they could, were forced to wait in line behind the majors when, towards the end of the 1940s, colour was more and more in demand. Technicolor began to get a reputation for being uncooperative and generally difficult, and it was precisely at this time that the anti-trust suit was brought against it (part of a wave of anti-trust actions and legislation that profoundly affected the industry overall, leading eventually to a split between production and distribution, the destruction of vertical integration, and finally to the more atomised and fragmented system we have today). The courts found against Technicolor, and ordered the company to set aside a certain number of cameras on a first-come first-served to non-major producers and studios. The decision appears to have had little impact upon Technicolor's future development. However it was, at the very least, symptomatic of shifts taking place within the industry which were, in turn, to shift Technicolor's position within it, and its own relationship to the general field of mass entertainment.

17. Jacobs, **The Rise of the American Film**, p. 447

## The Advent of Eastman Color

The introduction of Eastman Color by Eastman Kodak changed markedly Technicolor's place within the colour field, leading first to modifications in Technicolor's practices, technologies and services and eventually, in the 1960s, to a policy of diversification, in which the company expanded its operations to include not only films but television (and not only colour, but also black-and-white). Eastman Color was a development of the German Agfa-color single-strip process. Its hallmark was that the three strips of colour sensitive film needed for the production of a colour image were bonded together in a single, tri-pack roll. Henceforth, a colour film could be shot on an ordinary one-lens camera, while in principle any laboratory with conventional processing facilities could produce colour prints. Technicolor's monopoly, based on its special camera and on its processing services, was henceforth a thing of the past. Eastman Kodak offered not only negative tri-pack film, but also colour positive and internegative stock as well. Within two or three years, nearly every major studio had adopted Eastman Color negative, while a number used the whole colour series. As the studios adopted and adapted the Eastman Color process, a new series of commercial brand names for colour processes used by the studios began to appear and proliferate: WarnerColor, Ansco Color, TruColor, De Luxe and so on. And this at precisely the point at which television was beginning to have a major impact on the industry, the point at which colour began more and more to be used in film as an attraction *vis-à-vis* TV's black-and-white, and the point at which widescreen, 3-D, and other technical developments and novelties were to be used (in conjunction with colour) to intensify the spectacle of cinema in general, the primary means by which the cinema sought to counteract the threat that television posed. An article written by Frederick Foster for **The American Cinematographer** in 1953, for instance, noted that Eastman Color was being used in particular 'in the production of many three-dimensional films, where 3-D cameras taking single film strips are employed instead of Technicolor's 3-strip cameras'[18] and that 'Twentieth Century-Fox studio is using Eastman color negative in its cameras in the production of CinemaScope films.'[19]

In fact, the value of colour to the film industry fluctuated during the 1950s and 1960s as the relationship of the industry to television, and as the importance of colour within television, themselves shifted and changed. The use of colour in film production increased steadily from 1935 to 1955, accelerating in particular during the early 1950s until colour films comprised some 50 per cent of total US output. As cinema audiences continued to dwindle despite the increasing emphasis on spectacle and technical gimmickry, the industry began negotiating with the television companies for the use of its product, and, as television was still in black-and-white, the commercial value of colour began consequently to decline:

> *Despite the fact that Eastman Color had increased the supply of color and cut some of the production costs, color feature film production declined in the mid-1950s while black-and-white production increased.*[20]

It was only during the mid-1960s, when television had converted to colour, that the use of colour in the cinema became virtually universal.

18. Frederick Foster, 'Eastman Negative-Positive Color Films for Motion Pictures', **The American Cinematographer**, July 1953, p. 322

19. Foster, 'Eastman Negative-Positive Color Films for Motion Pictures', p. 332

20. Kindem, 'Hollywood's Conversion to Color', p. 34

Clearly, the introduction of Eastman Color had substantial effects on Technicolor, establishing Eastman Kodak's importance within the field of colour technology. Technicolor, however, maintained a modified but still substantially hegemonic position. It continued to supply release prints and modified its processing techniques to accommodate the demands of wide-screen systems. In consequence, **The Robe,** the first CinemaScope film, was shot and processed by Technicolor, as was **White Christmas,** the first film in VistaVision. Technicolor manufactured the prints for **This is Cinerama** and itself introduced such wide-screen formats as Technirama and Technirama-70. With the opening of a television film processing plant in 1965, Technicolor's relationship with the television industry was cemented. As television itself adopted colour, meanwhile, the aesthetic value of colour in the cinema began to change. As colour began to be used on television for news and current affairs programmes, the overwhelming association of colour with fantasy and spectacle began to be weakened: colour acquired instead the value of realism. Realism, however, was one of the discourses used to support and motivate the use of colour in the cinema in the first place. This contradiction, and the discourses of fantasy and spectacle, on the one hand, and of realism, on the other, are worth discussing in more detail, in the context of a general consideration of the aesthetics and ideology of colour in film.

# 9:

## Colour and Film Aesthetics

### Colour, Realism and Spectacle

In an article entitled 'Sound and Color', Edward Buscombe has discussed the extent to which an ideology of realism has dictated debates about technology in the cinema, not only with respect to sound and colour, but also with respect to CinemaScope, 3-D and so on:

*Economic theories can only partially explain technological innovations, since economics cannot say why innovations take the form they do, only why they are an essential part of the system. Economics can explain the necessary but not the sufficient conditions for innovation. No new technology can be introduced unless the economic system requires it. But a new technology cannot be successful unless it fulfils some kind of need. The specific form of this need will be ideologically determined; in the case of cinema the ideological determinant most frequently identified has been: realism.*[1]

Buscombe then goes on, however, to note that when colour first became technically feasible, it tended to connote, not reality, but fantasy. Because colour was initially associated with fantasy and spectacle its use tended to be restricted to genres like the cartoon, the western, the costume romance and the musical rather than the war film, the documentary and the crime picture. More than that, though, colour was a *problem* for realism because colour could distract and disturb the eye. Buscombe quotes Douglas Fairbanks' comments on colour after making **The Black Pirate** in 1927:

1. Edward Buscombe, 'Sound and Color', Jump Cut, no. 17, p. 24

*Not only has the process of color motion picture photography never been perfected, but there has been a grave doubt whether, even if properly developed, it could be applied, without detracting more than it added to motion picture technic. The argument has been that it would tire and distract the eye, taking attention from acting, and facial expression, blur and confuse the action. In short it has been felt that it would militate against the simplicity and directness which motion pictures derive from the unobtrusive black and white.*[2]

Colour would, or could, 'serve only to distract the audience from those elements in the film which carried forward the narrative: acting, facial expression, "the action". The unity of the diegesis and the primacy of the narrative are fundamental to realist cinema. If color was seen to threaten either one it could not be accommodated'.[3] Buscombe goes on to quote from **Elements of Color in Professional Motion Pictures,** an industry manual published in 1957. The manual indeed argues that the use of colour must be carefully motivated, subordinated to the story and 'the action': 'the objective being to have color "act" with the story, never being a separate entity to compete with or detract from the dramatic content of the picture'.[4] There are exceptions to the rule of realism, however, and these include the use of colour in musicals and fantasy films:

*Musicals and fantasy pictures are open to unlimited opportunities in the creative use of color. Here we are not held down by reality, past or present, and our imaginations can soar. Musicals and fantasies are usually designed to provide the eye with visual pleasure in the way that music pleases the ear.*[5]

Colour can be used 'creatively' in those genres whose rules of verisimilitude are not tied to conventions of realism in the way that other genres, like the war film and the documentary may be. Colour can be used 'creatively' in genres 'designed to provide the eye with visual pleasure'. Colour can similarly be used in the visual presentation of the female star:

*The feminine star . . . whose appearance is of paramount importance, must be given undisputed priority as to the color of make-up, hair and costume which will best complement her complexion and her figure. If her complexion limits the colors she can wear successfully, this in turn restricts the background colours which will complement her complexion and her costumes to best advantage.*[6]

The basic potential contradiction to which Buscombe refers in the use and discussion of colour during the decades which saw its gradual diffusion throughout the industry and its range of

2. Buscombe, 'Sound and Color', p. 24

3. Buscombe, 'Sound and Color', p. 24

4. Buscombe, 'Sound and Color', p. 24

5. Buscombe, 'Sound and Color', p. 25

6. Buscombe, 'Sound and Color', p. 25

basic genres, is the contradiction between colour as an index of realism and colour as a mark of fantasy, as an element capable, therefore, of disrupting or detracting from the very realism it is otherwise held to inscribe. The contradiction is by no means absolute. It is one which is managed, contained, in a number of different ways. One of the most persistent of these has been to combine a discourse of reality with a discourse of art and artifice. Colour is valued both because it is a 'natural' ingredient of visual reality *and* because it lends itself to artistic effects. Thus alongside a discourse in which Technicolor can advertise itself with the slogan 'Technicolor *is* natural color' or in which a Kinemacolor programme can describe the Kinemacolor process as 'The GREATEST INVENTION of the CENTURY Reflecting Nature in her ACTUAL COLORS', there is a discourse which constantly invokes artifice, art and, especially, the paintings of the 'Old Masters'. The Technicolor advertisement quoted above, in addition to invoking nature, contains the claim that 'Technicolor has *painted* for the millions of motion picture "fans" a new world'. (My emphasis.) **The Gulf Between,** the early Technicolor film, was described by **Motion-Picture News** in the following terms:

> *unquestionably the finest natural color picture ever produced. The process . . . results in the absence of all 'fringe', absence of eye strain and produces colors that are really natural. The invitation audience . . . was moved time and again to burst into applause of the sort that lasted long. The final shot, showing the sun setting over the water is beautiful — mindful of a Japanese painting.*[7]

The **New York Times** noted that in **The Black Pirate** (1926), 'The unrivalled beauty of the different episodes is mindful of the paintings of the old masters'.[8] The **Hollywood Reporter** described the use of colour in **Ramona** as follows:

> *This picture in color raises the artistic status of the screen by several degrees. It will be acclaimed the most beautiful motion picture ever filmed . . . The color goes beyond anything previously achieved. Not only has the Technicolor process yielded truer values, more transparent shadows, closer uniformity, and sharper definition, but the use of color in costumes, properties, background, and make-up shows a vastly finer taste and artistry.*[9]

Much was made of pictorial references to painters like Murillo, Goya and El Greco in Rouben Mamoulian's **Blood and Sand** (1941). Mamoulian himself explained that:

> *After all, in making a motion picture, and especially in making a motion picture in color, we are essentially making a series of paintings. What does it matter if we are not painting our picture*

7. Quoted in Basten, **Glorious Technicolor,** pp. 26–7

8. Quoted in Basten, **Glorious Technicolor,** p. 37

9. Quoted in Basten, **Glorious Technicolor,** p. 74

with water color or oil paint, but with colored light projected on a white screen? What does it matter if our picture moves and speaks? It is still fundamentally a picture. To what better source of inspiration could we turn than to the greatest masters of painting?[10]

10. Quoted in Basten, *Glorious Technicolor*, p. 127

Meanwhile, from a different perspective, Carl Dreyer, in discussing the use of colour in film, was to bemoan the lack of genuinely 'aesthetic' colour films:

> How many of them do we remember for the aesthetic pleasure they give us? Two-three-four-five? Possibly five — but probably no more. Castellani's **Romeo and Juliet** *(1953) just manages to be among them — after Olivier's* **Henry V** *and Kinugasa's* **Gate of Hell**. *Olivier got his ideas for his color schemes from the illuminated manuscripts of the period. Kinugasa got his from the classical engravings of his people.*[11]

11. Carl Dreyer, 'Color and Color Films', in Lewis Jacobs (ed.), *The Movies as Medium* (New York: Farrar, Strauss & Giroux, 1970) p. 197

There is a shift, then, from nature to art. But there is also a shift, evident in these quotations, from a reference to art as a means of evoking and describing some of the effects produced by colour in excess of realism, to a reference to films which reproduce certain painterly styles not only to produce those effects, but also to organise and contain them. The effects in themselves are capable of producing the kinds of irritation and disturbance to which Fairbanks refers. Once organised and contained, once composed, though, they are also capable of producing the 'aesthetic pleasure', the 'visual pleasure' to which Dreyer and the manual Buscombe quotes respectively refer. The function of organising, composing and controlling those effects was not solely provided by borrowing styles and devices direct from the visual arts. It was provided more generally by those rules and techniques devised both in theory and practice for the subordination of colour to 'the unity of the diegesis and the primacy of narrative'. It was provided too by the rules and conventions governing the relative balance between narrative, on the one hand, and spectacle, on the other, since what colour tended to provide, above all else, was spectacle.

Hence the generic variation to which Buscombe refers, where colour tended to be accommodated much more easily by the cartoon and the musical than by the war film and documentary. Hence too the ways in which colour sequences tended to be used in films early on. In von Stroheim's **The Wedding March** (1929), for instance, a two-colour process was used to film a military parade. As the parade and sequence begin the narrative comes to a halt, and spectacle takes over. A similar use of colour in sequences is apparent in the early musicals. Motivation for the abandonment of narrative in favour of spectacle is provided by the musical numbers themselves. It was generally during the course of these numbers that colour was used.

Guy Green, a cinematographer working in Britain, writing in the late 1940s, indicates the extent to which colour was identified with spectacle — and the extent to which both colour and spectacle were potentially problematic in conventional realist drama. Having discussed the properties and potentials of colour, Green proceeds as follows:

> *The obvious question arising out of this is: why not use these properties of colour photography deliberately, and the answer is simple. No one has yet found a completely satisfactory method. In one field it is used with great success — the musical. The Americans with consummate technical skill exploit colour's advantages over monochrome to the full and give us a dazzling and often breathtaking eyeful, and the colour is part of the show.*
>
> *Photography for dramatic subjects cannot be approached in this way. It must reflect the emotional content of the screen. It must help the audience forget that they are in a cinema at all. It must not be a glorious spectacle all on its own. Therefore in some way it must be suppressed and made to lend itself to the subject dramatically.*[12]

Similarly, Major Cornwell-Clyne, writing at the same time, notes that one of the major factors in antagonistic public reaction to colour centres on the extent to which colour 'attracts their attention from the "story"'.[13] He goes on, like Guy Green, to discuss the use of colour, the problem of colour, in the 'dramatic film':

> *In the majority of films the material is principally concerned with dramatic episodes interpreted in terms of the motion picture technique. The subject of most pictures, namely, the focus of attention, is certainly not upon colour. When the audience's attention is diverted from the action of the drama, or from the drama in action, by a colour incident, arrangement or phenomenon, then such colour is an intruder destroying the unity of the film and usurping the proper functioning of other more important elements of the film dynamics.*[14]

Clyne proceeds then to elaborate what he himself terms 'a law':

> <u>*Colour should never attract the attention without carrying a significance necessary for the more complete presentation to the observer of the unfoldment of the drama.*</u>
>
> *The observer should never be conscious of colour at all until it means something.*[15]

---

12. Quoted in John Huntley, **British Technicolor Films** (London: Skelton Robinson, 1949) pp. 117–8

13. Major A. Cornwell-Clyne, 'What's Wrong With Colour?' in Huntley, **British Technicolor Films**, p. 194

14. Cornwell-Clyne, 'What's Wrong With Colour?', p. 194

15. Cornwell-Clyne, 'What's Wrong With Colour?', p. 194

These comments highlight both the extent to which colour as a spectacle was itself, however motivated, composed and controlled, to some extent incompatible with narrative and drama, and the extent to which, in any case, such motivation, composition and control was essential: 'The observer must never be conscious of colour at all unless it means something'. Technicolor, of course, was always very much aware of the need for such control. For many years, through the agency of Natalie Kalmus, who acted as Technicolor's colour consultant, the use of colour in film was subject to a very strict and particular aesthetic regulation. Kalmus always worked very closely on the design of colour in Technicolor's films:

*The script of every film is sent to her beforehand, and she prepares a colour chart, scientifically planned and thoroughly detailed. Colour, material blending, types of materials, paints and floor coverings are just a few of the items dealt with at length.*[16]

16. John K. Newman, 'Profile of Natalie Kalmus', in Huntley, **British Technicolor Films**, p. 148

Her stated ideology on the place and use of colour in film, because of her position an extremely important and influential one, is the conventional mixture of realism and art: colour as an index of reality and a source of aesthetic effects:

*Motion pictures have been steadily tending towards complete realism. In the early days, pictures were a mere mechanical process of imprinting light upon film and projecting that result upon the screen. Then came the perfection of detail — more accurate sets and costumes — more perfect photography. The advent of sound brought increased realism through the auditory sense. The last step — colour, with the addition of chromatic sensations — completed the process. Now motion pictures are able to duplicate faithfully all the auditory and visual sensations.*

*This enhanced realism enables us to portray life and nature as it really is, and in this respect we have made definite strides forward. A motion picture, however, will be merely an accurate record of certain events unless we guide this realism into the realms of art. To accomplish this it becomes necessary to augment the mechanical processes with the inspirational work of the artist. It is not enough that we put a perfect record on the screen. That record must be moulded according to the basic principles of art.*[17]

17. Natalie Kalmus, 'Colour', in Stephen Watts (ed.), **Behind the Screen** (London: Arthur Barker, 1938) p. 116

She goes on to concisely delineate the principle of motivation in the use of colour and its effects in order to join together the twin poles of reality and art:

*When we receive the script for a new film, we carefully analyse each sequence and scene to ascertain what dominant mood or emotion is to be expressed. When this is decided, we plan to use the appropriate colour or set of colours which will suggest that mood, thus actually* fitting the colour to the scene and augmenting its dramatic value.[18]

Colour is 'fitted' to the scene. It 'augments' its 'dramatic value'. Like the use of tinting and toning, colour is determined by the 'dominant mood or emotion' (though because a spectrum of colours is available the rhetoric involved in a strategy of this kind is much less evident; it is motivated, in its turn, by the 'realism' of colour cinematography). The use of colour is at all points aesthetically motivated. It is subordinate to the narrative, the drama, the diegesis rather than being an autonomous element. Finally,

*Unless the dramatic aspect dictates to the contrary, it is desirable to have all the colours in any one scene harmonious. Otherwise, we strike an unpleasant, discordant note.*[19]

Kalmus' views were not idiosyncratic. They were perfectly consonant with the aesthetic views and practices of Hollywood as a whole with respect to colour and its use (as the quotations cited above amply testify). With some modification they are still prevalent today. Where her views (and those of Technicolor in general) were contravened, as for instance when John Huston used colour filters in shooting **Moulin Rouge,** they were contravened in minor detail. And significantly, in this particular instance, the contravention was motivated by the wish to evoke and refer to the style of a painter, Toulouse Lautrec. We are back again with spectacle, art and the organisation of colour's effects.

## Colour and the Female Image

Thus a constellation of terms are used to refer to and to prescribe the presence and the use of colour in film. Nature, realism, spectacle and art recur as the key terms within a discourse about colour, its use and its effects. This discourse and these terms function so as to negotiate in theory (and then in practice) some of the contradictions involved in using colour and some of the effects it can produce. These effects can exceed either nature and realism on the one hand or spectacle and art on the other (just as spectacle and art can exceed both narrative and drama). Neither the one set of terms nor the other seems capable, on their own, of containing fully, in descriptive terms, some of the effects to which they refer. Moreover, there is in any case at first glance a clear contradiction

[18]. Kalmus, 'Colour', p. 121. My emphasis
[19]. Kalmus, 'Colour', p. 123

between them. It is at this point that a further element, one which is just as constant, just as persistent, enters into the ideological equation. That element is the female body. Since women within patriarchal ideology already occupy the contradictory spaces both of nature and culture (since they therefore evoke both the natural and the artificial) and since also they are marked as socially sanctioned objects of erotic looking, it is no wonder that from the earliest days of colour photography they function both as a source of the spectacle of colour in practice and as a reference point for the use and promotion of colour in theory. The female body both bridges the ideological gap between nature and cultural artifice while simultaneously marking and focusing the scopophilic pleasures involved in and engaged by the use of colour in film.

As evidence, one might first point to the enormous number of early colour photographs which depict not just women, but women either in natural settings or posed in a studio with plants and flowers: 'Old Familiar Flowers' (1919), 'Nude' (1912), 'Grecian Study' (1913), 'The Rose Arbour' (1914), 'Girl with Flowers' (1913), 'The Two Friends' (1927), 'Portrait of a Girl' (1916), 'Lady in an Orange Dress' (1915) and 'Molly Mulligan' (1914). (These in addition both to simple colour portraits on the one hand and to pictures like 'La Vulgarisation' (1909) on the other.)

Moving from the field of colour photography to colour in film, one can quote Eisenstein's description of some of the early colour films he saw in Riga:

*The coloured short films always seemed to have a pinkish tone, whether they showed the white sails of yachts skimming over the ultramarine sea, or variously colored fruits and flowers arranged by girls with flaming red or straw-yellow hair.*[20]

Or Technicolor's 1930 advertisement, 'If rainbows were black and white', which begins

*Suppose that, since the world began, rainbows had been black and white! And flowers; and trees; Alpine sunsets; the Grand Canyon and the Bay of Naples; the eyes and lips and hair of pretty girls!*

Cinematographer Ray Rennahan, in giving his views about the effect of colour films on the depiction of the female body, interweaves the terms and discourses of nature and art: 'beauty', like 'woman', is both natural and artificial. Rennahan argues for a new balance between the two, a shift away from the forms of artifice marking the depiction of women in black-and-white films:

*I consider that the coming of colour will mark a return of*

20. Sergei Eisenstein, 'One Path to Color', in Lewis Jacobs (ed.), **The Movies as Medium**, pp. 201–2

naturalness in screen heroines. The reason is that Technicolor requires a very light make-up. An actress appearing before a colour camera could walk off the set into the street — and if her make-up were commented on it would probably be described as insufficient! Consequently the days of painting the lily are likely to pass. Natural beauty will be at a premium. Beauty that relies on the make-up expert will be under a cloud.[21]

21. Quoted in Huntley, **British Technicolor Films**, p. 25

What this does not acknowledge is the degree of artifice necessary for the production of 'natural beauty' and the place both of Technicolor and of the female star in the production of 'glamour'. Rennahan's remarks about make-up can be counter-pointed both with the extent to which the arrival of Technicolor required a change in make-up techniques and in the production of make-up itself (a change in part consequent upon the extent to which, as Rennahan's remarks symptomatically suggest, colour accompanied and produced a new regime of female 'beauty') and with his own subsequent remarks, which indicate the extent to which the new 'natural beauty' in combination with the qualities of Technicolor as a process excluded certain types of 'natural' colouring. During the mid-1930s, Max Factor produced a new range of make-up expressly for use in Technicolor films, basing it upon a 'cake' rather than a paste or greasepaint format. Max Factor himself pointed to the complexities (the artifice) involved:

> Previous make-ups were based on various combinations of pink, yellow and white. Well applied, they may have looked very nice to the eye but the more critical color camera unmasks it for the glaringly unnatural thing it is. In analyzing the human complexion with a spectroscope, we found that the darker pinks, or red, are present as well as certain proportions of yellow, white and blue. This is true because the skin itself is essentially a translucent covering with very little color of its own. So our new make-up had to be made to blend with not one but a number of colors.[22]

22. Quoted in Basten, **Glorious Technicolor**, p. 71

Factor went on to note some of the changes in practice colour involved:

> In black-and-white we worked with contrasts of light and shade. When making up a blonde, for example, we sought to heighten that tonal contrast by applying a rather dark make-up which gave a positive contrast to the light hair. In color, this is not the case. A blonde or brunette would use a make-up of a color in keeping with her own complexion . . . We are no longer striving for a purely artificial contrast but seeking to imitate and enhance the subject's natural coloring.[23]

23. Quoted in Basten, **Glorious Technicolor**, p. 71

Rennahan, meanwhile, specifies both some of the

components of the new 'natural beauty' — and some of the 'natural' colours it nevertheless excluded:

> *The most important quality in a color star is a perfect skin. It should be clear and delicately colored. The technicolor process is exacting; in a close-up in this process even the pores are visible.*
>
> *Next in importance is a distinct shade of hair. Mid-colours are difficult. Black, though often beautiful, is difficult to light. Platinum blonde is 'out' — the most difficult shade of all to photograph and useless for Technicolor. It is already going by the board in Hollywood.*[24]

[24. Quoted in Basten, **Glorious Technicolor**, p. 25]

'Natural beauty', for all its contradictions, was nevertheless a constant in discourses linking together Technicolor and the female body:

> *Most heartening, perhaps, were the reactions to the color camera's treatment of the female lead. Wrote one critic: 'Loretta Young, the most appealing of the screen's ladies, wears a black wig, photographs beautifully in natural colors.'*
>
> *Another notes: 'Loretta Young ... is graced by the Technicolor camera in a mood of idyllic beauty ... Color close-ups of Miss Young are breathtaking gems.'*[25]

[25. Basten, **Glorious Technicolor**, p. 76]

As mentioned above, the discourse of 'natural beauty' existed alongside, in combination with, the discourse of 'glamour'. Here the extent to which the spectacle of colour in combination with the spectacle of the female body involved an explicitly eroticised male look was perhaps much more explicitly recognised:

> *To film fans, particularly during Hollywood's 'glory years', Technicolor meant glamor, spectacle and excitement.*[26]

[26. Robert Surtees, 'Forward' to Basten, **Glorious Technicolor**, p. 9]

> *During the filming of* **Gone With the Wind,** *cinematographer Ernest Haller remarked, 'Whenever an established feminine star makes her first appearance in a color film the critics almost always exclaim at great length about the new personality color gives her.*
>
> *'Now that we have this fast film, which enables a cinematographer to use all the little tricks of precision lighting he has used in monochrome to glamorize his stars, I am sure that color is going to be more flattering than ever to women.'*[27]

[27. Basten, **Glorious Technicolor**, p. 102]

> *Betty Grable in Technicolor is balm for the eyes.*[28]

[28. **New York Times** review of **Wabash Avenue,** plate caption in Basten, **Glorious Technicolor**, p. 111]

> *It was wartime and there were millions of American G.I.'s around the world who wanted nothing more than to have lovely, talented ladies entertain them. Movies were a touch of*

*home, and there were few things that pleased the men in the Armed Forces more than a Technicolor movie filled with attractive females.*

*The timing was perfect. Technicolor had managed to glorify the leading lady just when she was about to be in big demand. The combination of Technicolor and beautiful girls was hard to resist.*[29]

Whether conceived and articulated in terms of the discourse of 'natural beauty' or the discourse of 'glamour', what was in any case both crucial and central was the inextricable interrelationship between colour (specifically Technicolor) and the image of the female body within the particular regime of representation and spectacle which the advent of colour brought to mainstream cinema:

*Arlene Dahl was called 'the girl for whom Technicolor was invented'. She had red-gold hair, bright blue eyes, a flawless complexion, and two heart-shaped beauty marks — one above the corner of her mouth, the other on her shoulder.*[30]

*Maureen O'Hara was crowned 'Queen of Technicolor' after only a few appearances before the color camera. What sounds like a publicist's inspiration came instead from the Technicolor Corporation itself, which used test footage of her during the early 1940s to help sell their process to the studios.*[31]

*Try to imagine* **Gone With The Wind** *without Technicolor. Or* **Fantasia.** *Or* **Ben-Hur.** *Or Betty Grable.*[32]

[29. Basten, **Glorious Technicolor**, p. 102]
[30. Basten, **Glorious Technicolor**, p. 122]
[31. Basten, **Glorious Technicolor**, p. 113]
[32. Surtees, 'Forword', p. 9]

## The Dimensions of Colour

The role of the female body within the regime of representation inaugurated by the introduction of Technicolor was one both of focusing and motivating a set of colour effects within a system dependent upon plot and narration, thus providing a form of spectacle compatible with that system, and of marking and containing the erotic component involved in the desire to look at the coloured image. Colour was capable of disturbing that system. It requires careful control and regulation. That requirement was met both by the forms of aesthetic motivation described by Natalie Kalmus and others (including those provided by styles of painting and graphic art) and by the forms of visual treatment of the female body. This is not to say that those effects were ever fully controlled or that the subjective and erotic processes involved in and engaged by looking at coloured images were ever fully contained. Precisely what those effects were or what those processes involved is difficult to specify. Colour has rarely been discussed outside the parameters of an 'objective' discourse, on the one hand, and a 'subjective' discourse on the other. The 'objective' discourse simply links colour to the objects in reality which provide its point of reference. Colour in film, or in other forms of visual representation, is seen simply as a reflection of the colour involved in the perception of those objects. The 'subjective' discourse is concerned to explore the reactions of individual subjects to various different colours. The two discourses are linked together in those various attempts which have been made to establish and to codify the 'meanings' of different colours (where those 'meanings' are viewed as either culturally specific or as in some senses universal). The problem here tends to be the over-rigid ascription of meaning, the attempt to reduce colour or colours to specific, verbalisable phrases or words or, at best, clusters of phrases and words. Each discourse, on its own, tends to operate a form of reduction. By contrast Julia Kristeva's writings on colour in painting have attempted to recognise each of these dimensions and elements. It is worth, therefore, by way of conclusion, looking more closely at what she has to say in an attempt to map out a set of conceptual parameters within which the effects and processes involved in the use of colour in film can begin to be discussed.

Kristeva sees colour as articulated across what she calls a 'triple register'. This triple register is comprised of the pressure exerted by psychic drives in relation to external objects; that same pressure as it arises from and is articulated across the body; and signification: 'The triple register is made up of a pressure marking an outside, another linked to the body proper, and a sign'.[33] She goes on to relate this register to colour:

*Color can be defined, considering what I have just said, as being articulated on such a triple register within the domain of visual perception: an instinctual pressure linked to external objects; the same pressure causing the eroticizing of the body proper via visual perception and gesture; and the insertion of this pressure under the impact of censorship as a sign in a system of representation.*[34]

Colour, then, is neither purely subjective nor purely objective. Nor are its meanings simply a matter of cultural convention. It is instead a complex phenomenon involving all three levels or factors simultaneously, the objective ('external

33. Julia Kristeva, **Desire in Language** (New York: Columbia University Press, 1980) p. 218

34. Kristeva, **Desire in Language**, p. 219

objects'), the subjective ('an instinctual pressure . . . causing the eroticization of the body') and the cultural ('the insertion of this pressure under the impact of censorship as a sign in a system of representation'):

> *Thence color, in each instance, must be deciphered according to: 1) the scale of 'natural' colors; 2) the psychology of color perception and, especially, the psychology of each perceptions's instinctual cathexis . . . and 3) the pictorial system either operative or in the process of formation.*[35]

Colour is thus — above all — a complex and composite element:

> *A preeminently composite element, color condenses 'objectivity', 'subjectivity', and the intrasystematic organization of pictorial practice. It thus emerges as a grid (of differences in light, energetic charge, and systematic value) whose every element is linked with several interlocking registers.*[36]

It could be noted at this point that this 'condensation' is most acute in colour photography and cinematography. 'Objectivity' is inscribed much more markedly into the photographic and cinematic image than it is into even the most realistic of painted images. Conversely, 'subjectivity' is less heavily marked. And within mainstream cinema, at least, the symbolic organisation of colour tends to be heavily motivated. All the efforts of a Natalie Kalmus were directed towards the motivation of colour systems, their subordination not just to narrative, but also to the referential properties of the cinematic image. Only on the fringes of Art Cinema (in some of the films of Antonioni, Godard and Resnais) and within the field of independent and avant-garde film have the symbolic properties of colour been explored to the full. This is not to argue, though, either that the 'intrasystematic organization' of colour did not exist in mainstream cinema or that there have not historically existed a distinct set of symbolic systems into which colour has been inserted. Kalmus' job was precisely to produce colour systems, not only for each film, but also for each scene and sequence within it, matching colour to mood and atmosphere and producing a mix and balance of colours appropriate to each particular segment. And one could point beyond the level of the organization of colour that she imposed to films which involve quite complex colour systems while remaining within the aesthetic and ideological ambit of 'realism': **The Cobweb, She Wore a Yellow Ribbon, Rebel Without a Cause, Written on the Wind,** and so on. One could point also to the differences (as well as the similarities) between 'natural' colour films and films involving tinting and toning. The latter inevitably involved a much more

---

35. Kristeva. **Desire in Language**, p. 219

36. Kristeva. **Desire in Language**, p. 219

heavily stylised rhetoric of colour, if only because the range of colours available within any one scene was heavily limited.

Kristeva goes on to argue that colour is capable of escaping, subverting and disrupting the symbolic organisation to which it is subject. Because it touches so centrally on the drives and pressures of the psyche in general and the unconscious in particular, it is capable of shattering the rules and laws to which it may be subject in any particular pictorial or cultural system. In this sense, colour

*achieves the momentary dialectic of law — the laying down of One Meaning so that it might at once be pulverized, multiplied into plural meanings. Color is the shattering of unity.*[37]

[37. Kristeva, **Desire in Language**, p. 221]

It is this aspect of colour that Hollywood, Technicolor, Natalie Kalmus sought to control. These were the effects that required organization. The capacity of colour to produce a 'pulverisation' of meaning, a multiplicity of meanings was marked, recognised and contained through the construction of colour systems, the matching of colour to dramatic mood, on the one hand, and to the referential exigencies of landscape, décor and so on the other. Cornwell-Clyne's dictum that the observer 'should never be conscious of colour at all until it means something' should perhaps then be slightly amended. The danger was not so much meaninglessness but rather an over abundance of contrary meanings. Colour ought only to bear the 'significance necessary'. No more, no less.

# Conclusion

The shape of this book is one that will doubtless be familiar from other, more conventional accounts of film technology and its history: first the still, photographic image, then the moving image, projected on to a screen, then sound, then colour. The shape tends to follow the chronology of technical innovation in the cinema. It is one that can easily lend itself (*has* easily lent itself) to two kinds of approaches, both of which I have tried here to question, if only implicitly. One approach, typified perhaps by James Limbacher's book, **Four Aspects of the Film,** is to treat technology as a self-contained sphere with a self-contained history. One technological event is preceded or followed by another, in simple chronological sequence. Each new feature or process either displaces those already in existence or else simply adds to them, increasing the stock of technical resources available. There are no real determinations on this process. Aesthetic, economic, legal or political facts and factors will from time to time be acknowledged and discussed. But they will tend to be accounted for in piecemeal fashion and at a purely local level, thus in effect depriving them of any general, systematic significance.

The second approach, far from refusing a central role to aesthetics, in particular, is one which is totally guided by the tenets of one particularly aesthetic, that of realism. According to this aesthetic, films reflect (or should reflect) reality. Working from the premise that the sounds and images comprising films are linked ontologically to the objects that the microphone and camera record, a few short steps (and a number of conceptual elisions) lead inexorably to the conclusion, elaborated by Bazin, Kracauer, Pasolini and others, that films themselves are inherently realist and that their language is the language of reality.[1] The

---

1. See André Bazin, 'The Ontology of the Photographic Image', 'The Myth of Total Cinema' and 'The Evolution of Film Language', in **What is Cinema?** (Berkeley: University of California Press, 1967); Siegfried Kracaeuer, **Theory of Film** (New York: Oxford University Press, 1960); and Oswald Stack, **Pasolini on Pasolini** (London: Thames & Hudson, 1969)

place of technology within this argument is crucial but contradictory. It is cinema's technology that guarantees its ontological basis: the microphone and camera enable the recording and transcription of the aural and visual world. But on the other hand, technology is an embarrassment, a hindrance, since it intervenes (of necessity) between the spectator and the pro-filmic event (that which the camera and microphone record). The history of technology in the cinema is seen as the history of an ever greater approximation to reality, with sound, colour, widescreen and the rest adding to the basic visual ontology. More and more technology is added, but the goal would be its complete disappearance, a technology that vanished as it performed its ultimate task. This approach, with its notion of a transparent cinematic language, represses not only the work of representation and technology, it represses also that which produces the films, the film industry.

While taking the same broad areas as a focus for discussion — the moving image, sound, colour, and so on — I have tried to develop a counter-approach, one in which a series of technological events and innovations are located within a variety of contexts — aesthetic, ideological and economic as well as scientific and technical. Each context, each set of factors are as important as the others. Technology in the cinema is reducible to none of these factors singly. It is instead the complex product of all of them. The one factor — or rather the one institution — that binds these other other factors together is the film industry. It is within the context provided by the industry and its practices at any one point in time that the precise articulation of these other factors takes place.

The adoption of examples and areas familiar from conventional accounts of film technology and its history, together with the limitations in scope inherent in a book of this size, have prevented both the discussion of other, less familiar examples and areas and the treatment in depth of factors and aspects mentioned only in passing. It would be interesting and important, for instance, to dicuss the history of the development of film stock, the history and practices of the film laboratories, and the precise effects of the technologies I have discussed upon the division of labour in film production. It would be important, too, to produce a systematic account of the effects of technological developments within the mainstream film industry upon alternative and oppositional practices of cinema. I hope that future work on film technology stems as much from absences such as these as from discussion of the arguments and examples specifically included in this book.

# Bibliography

Armes, R., *Film and Reality* (Harmondsworth: Penguin, 1974).
Baiblé, C.; Marie, M.; Ropars, M.C., *Muriel* (Paris: Editions Galilée, 1974).
Balio, T. (ed.), *The American Film Industry* (Wisconsin: The University of Wisconsin Press, 1976).
Basten, F.E., *Glorious Technicolor* (London: A.S. Barnes, 1980).
Bazin, A., *What is Cinema?*, vol. 1 (Berkeley: University of California Press, 1967).
Burch, N., *To the Distant Observer* (London: Scolar Press, 1979).
Cameron, E.W. (ed.), *Sound and the Cinema* (New York: Redgrave Publishing Company, 1980).
Chanan, M., *The Dream that Kicks* (London, Boston & Henley: Routledge & Kegan Paul, 1980).
Coe, B., *The Birth of Photography* (London: Ash & Grant, 1976).
Coe, B., *Colour Photography, the First 100 Years, 1840–1940* (London: Ash & Grant, 1978).
Collett, J. (ed.) *Lectures du Film* (Paris: Albatross, 1975).
Conant, M., *Antitrust in the Motion Picture Industry* (Berkeley and Los Angeles: University of California Press, 1960).
Coustet, E., *Le Cinéma* (Paris, Hachette, 1921).
Deslandes, J., *Histoire générale du cinéma,* vol. 1 (Paris: Casterman, 1966–68).
Fielding, R. (ed.), *A Technological History of Motion Pictures and Television* (Berkeley: University of California Press, 1967).

Gernsheim, A. and Gernsheim, H., *The History of Photography* (London: Oxford University Press, 1955).

Gernsheim, A. and H., *L.J.M. Daguerre* (New York: Dover, 1968).

Gregory, R. L., *Eye and Brain* (London: Weidenfeld & Nicolson, 1966).

Hampton, B., *History of the American Film Industry* (New York: Dover, 1970).

Hendricks, G., *The Kinetoscope* (New York: Beginnings of the American Film, 1966).

Huntley, J., *British Technicolor Films* (London: Skelton Robinson, 1949).

Ivins, W. M., *Art and Geometry* (New York: Dover, 1964).

Jacobs, L., *The Rise of the American Film* (New York: Harcourt Brace, 1939).

Jacobs, L. (ed.), *The Movies as Medium* (New York: Farrar, Strauss & Giroux, 1970).

Klein, A.B., *Colour Cinematography* (London: Chapman & Hall, 1936).

Klingender, F. D. and Legg, S., *The Money Behind the Screen* (London: Lawrence & Wishart, 1937).

Kracauer, S., *Theory of Film* (New York: Oxford University Press, 1965).

Kristeva, J., *Desire in Language* (New York: Columbia University Press, 1980).

de Lauretis, T. and Heath, S. (eds.), *The Cinematic Apparatus* (London: Macmillan, 1980).

Limbacher, J.L., *Four Aspects of the Film* (New York: Brussell & Brussell, 1969).

Macdonald, G., *Camera: a Victorian Eyewitness* (London: Bastford, 1979).

Manvell, R. (ed.), *The International Encyclopaedia of Film* (London: Michael Joseph, 1972).

Mitry, J., *Histoire du Cinéma*, vol. 1 (Paris: Editions Universitaire, 1969).

Panofsky, E., *Renaissance and Renascences in Western Art* (New York, Hagerstown, San Francisco, London: Harper & Row, 1972).

Pinel, V., *Louis Lumière* (Paris: Anthologie du Cinéma, no. 78, 1974).

Pirenne, M.H., *Optics, Painting and Photography* (London: Cambridge University Press, 1970).

Pollack, P., *The Picture History of Photography* (New York: Abrams, 1969).

Pratt, G.C. (ed.), *Spellbound in Darkness,* vol. 1 (New York: University School of Liberal and Applied Studies, 1966).

Richter, G., *Perspective in Greek and Roman Art* (London: Phaidon, 1970).

Ryan, R. T., *A History of Motion Picture Colour Technology* (London and New York: Focal Press, 1977).

Sadoul, G., *Louis Lumière,* Cinéma d'Aujourd'hui (Paris: Editions Seghers, 1964).

Sadoul, G., *Histoire générale du cinéma* (Paris: Editions Denoël, 1948).

Scharf, A., *Art and Photography* (Harmondsworth: Pelican, 1974).

Scharf, A. (ed.), *Pioneers of Photography* (London: BBC, 1975).

Sontag, S., *On Photography* (London: Allen Lane, 1978).

Stack, O., *Pasolini on Pasolini* (London: Thames & Hudson, 1969).

Thomas, A., *The Expanding Eye* (London: Croom Helm, 1978).

Thomas, D. B., *The First Colour Motion Pictures* (London: HMSO, 1969).

Uspensky, B., *The Semiotics of the Russian Icon* (Ghent: Peter de Ridder Press, 1976).

Walker, A., *The Shattered Silents* (London: Elm Tree Books, 1978).

Watts, S. (ed.), *Behind the Screen* (London: Arthur Barker, 1938).

# Index

Actologue 92
**Adventures of Tom Sawyer, The** (1938) 136
Aeo-light 70
Agatograph 11
Agfacolor 142
Alberti, Leon Battista 12, 19
Alemann, Claudia 103
Alhazen 11
Allgemeine Elektrizitäts Gesellschaft (AEG) 83
American Telephone and Telegraph Company (AT&T) 75, 78, 85
**Anchors Away** 139
Animatograph 41
**Annabell's Butterfly Dance** 114
Anschütz, Ottomar 31, 40
Apollinaire, Guillaume 55
**Arabian Nights** (1942) 139
Arago, Dominique-François 29
Archer, Frederick Scott 33
Armat, Thomas 48
Armes, Roy 47
Armet, E. H. 64
Associated British 84
Associated Ltd 84
Associated Radio Pictures Company 84
Audion tube 65, 71

Bell, Joseph 129
**Bandit of Sherwood Forest, The** 139
Barker, Robert 26
Baucus, Joseph 44
Baudry, Jean-Louis 56
Bauer and Marshall 87
Bazin, André 159
Beal, L. S. 32
**Becky Sharp** 136
Bell, Alexander Graham 62
Bell and Howell camera 67, 70
Bell Telephone Company 71
**Ben Hur** (1960) 155
Benshi 92
Benson, Erastus 43
Berard, F. 29
Betaniorama 24
**Billy the Kid** 139
Bio-Fantascope 40
Biograph 49
Bioscope 31, 32, 41
**Birth of a Nation** 117

**Black Pirate, The** 132, 145, 147
Blake, E. V. 62
**Blind Spot** 103
**Blood and Sand** 147
Bonnelli 32
Bothamley, C. H. 38
Bouson, Charles-Marie 26
Breeze, Charles 38
Bristol, William 64
British Acoustic Films 68
British International 84
British Talking Picture Association 84
**Broadway Melody** 101, 133
**Broadway Rhythm** 139
Brunelleschi, Filippo 12, 13
**Buffalo Bill** 139
Buscombe, Edward 145, 146, 148

Calotype 32, 33
Camera lucida 10, 11, 29
Camera obscura 10–12, 20
Carbon arc lights 88
Carbutt, John 43
**Carnival Scenes at Nice and Cannes** 123
Case, Theodore W. 69–71, 75, 78
Casler, Herman 42, 43
Castellani 148
**Cat and the Fiddle, The** 136
Catchings, Waddill 83
Celluloid 43, 45, 47
Chanan, Michael 30, 31, 48, 49
Charles 11
Chase Manhattan Bank 85, 131
Child, H. L. 17
**Children's Battle of Flowers** 123
Choreutoscope 32
Chrètien, Gilles-Louis 11
Chronochrome 123–6, 129
Chronophotography 35–7, 51
**Church Parade of the 7th and 16th Lancers** 123
CinemaScope 143–5
Cinématographe 41, 45, 46, 50–2
Cinerama 127, 144
Claudet, Antoine 32
**Cobweb, The** 157
Coburn, Alvin Langdon 10
Cocteau, Jean 55
**Colonel Cody and his Sioux Indians** 50
**Colonel Cody's Shooting Skill** 50
Colorcraft 123

Columbia Broadcasting System  83
Commerz und Privat Bank  87
Comolli, Jean-Louis  56, 57, 100
Comstock, Daniel  129
Conant, Michael  49
**Congress Dances, The**  102
**Conversation, The**  40
Cook  32
Cooper, Meriam C.  136
Cooper-Hewitt mercury vapour lamp  126
Coppola, Francis Ford  103
Cornwell-Clyne, A.  149, 158
Cosmorama  24
Coustet, Ernest  126
Crawford, Merritt  77
Croft  40
Cyclorama  24
**Cytherea**  132

Daguerre, Louis  10, 21, 26, 27
Daguerrotype  20, 26, 32, 33
Dahl, Arlene  155
Damisch, Hubert  10, 20
Davies, Marion  117
De Forest, Lee  65, 68–70, 77
**Delhi Durbar**  123
De Luxe Color  140
DeMille, Cecil B.  117
**Desert Song, The** (1929)  101, 133
Deslandes, Jacques  3, 47
Diaphanorama  24–6
Dickson, W. K. L.  41–3, 46, 50
Digraph  11
Diorama  24, 26–8
Disdéri, Adolphe Eugène  21
Disney, Walt  136
Dissolving Views  39
Doane, Mary Ann  102
Dolby sound system  105
Donisthorpe, Wordsworth  40
**Don Juan**  73
Dramagraph  92
Dramatone  92
**Drei von der Tangstelle**  102
Dreyer, Carl  148
Dubosq, Jules  31, 32
Duddell oscillograph  76
**Dumbo**  139
Du Mont, Henry  32
Dupont  85

Eastman Color  142–4
Eastman, George  43
Eastman Kodak  118, 133, 137, 139–44
Edison, Thomas Alva  41–3, 46–50, 53, 54, 56, 63, 64, 78, 79, 114
Eidophusikon  24, 25, 28
Eisenstein, Sergei  152

Electrical Research Products Incorporated (ERPI)  70, 71, 78
Engl, Joseph  67
Equity and Law Life Assurance Society  87
Eugraph  11
Europerama  24

Factor, Max  153
Fairbanks, Douglas  117, 132, 145, 148
Famous Players-Lasky  132
**Fantasia**  155
Faraday, Michael  31
Fielding, Raymond  91
First National  81, 82, 85
**Flowers and Trees**  136
Foster, Frederick  143
Fox Film Corporation  71, 80, 82–5, 136, 143
Fox, William  71
Fox-Case Corporation  71
Fox-Loew  82, 83
Franklin, Chester  131
Fresnel, Augustin Jean  29

**Gaiety Girls, The**  50
Gainsborough Pictures  84
Goldman, Sachs  85
Gammon, Frank  44
**Gate of Hell**  148
Gaumont  68, 84, 124, 125
Gaumont, Léon  64, 78
Gaumont-Aubert-Franco Films  84, 87
Gaumont British Pictures  84, 87
Gemma-Frisius, Rainer  12
General Electric  47, 74–6, 85
General Motors  85
Gernsheim, Alison and Helmut  27
Giorama  24
**Glorious Adventure, The**  125
Godard, Jean-Luc  157
**Gold Diggers of Broadway, The**  133
Goldwyn Pictures  81, 85
Goldwyn, Samuel  132, 136
Gomery, Douglas  79
**Gone with the Wind**  136, 155
Goya, Francisco  147
Grable, Betty  154
Greco, El  147
Green, Guy  149
Griffith, D. W.  117

Hall, Hal  132
**Hallelujah**  101
Haller, Ernest  154
Handschiegl, Max  117
Handschiegl process  117
**Hearts of Dixie**  101
Heath, Stephen  17, 18

Heliograph 32
Helmholtz, Herman von 29, 111
Hendricks, Gordon 42
**Henry V** 148
Herschel, John 29, 31
Holland, Andrew 44
**Hollywood Revue** 101
Horner, William George 31
**House of Rothschild** 136
Hoxie, Charles 75
Humanova 92
**Hungarian Rhapsody** 102
Huston, John 151
Hyalograph 11

Ideal Renting Company 84
Illinois University 67
Imbibation process 132
**Intolerance** 117
Isensee, H. 114

**Joan the Woman,** 117
Jacobs, Lewis 137, 141
Janssen, Pierre Jules 34, 37
**Japanese Dances** 50
**Jazz Singer, The** 73
John F. Dryden-Prudential Insurance 85
Jolson, Al 73

Kalmus, Comstock and Wescott 140
Kalmus, Herbert 129, 131
Kalmus, Natalie 150, 151, 155, 157, 158
Kalorama 24
Kathodophone 67
Kelleycolor 123
Kellog, Edward 75, 77
Kelley, William van Doren 124, 125
Kennedy, Joseph 82
Kerr cell 76
**Kid Millions** 136
Kinchrome 123
Kindem, Gorham 136, 137, 139, 140
Kinemacolor 121–9, 147
Kinematograph 41–2, 46, 49
Kinematophone 92
Kinematoscope 32, 41–3, 46–51
Kineorama 24
Kinugasa 148
**Kismet** 139
Klångfilm 83
Klein, Adrian Bernard 135
Klingender, F. D. 85
König, Franz Niklaus 25
Kracauer, Siegfried 159
Kristeva, Julia 56, 156–8
Kromoscope 123
Kuchenmeisters Internationale Mij voor Sprekende Films 83

Kuchenmeisters Internationale Ultraphone Mij 83
Kuhn, Edmund 62
Kuhn, Loeb and Company 85
Kunz, Jacob 67

Laemmle, Carl 64, 78
Lampascope 24, 25
Lauste, Eugene 66, 67, 74, 77
Lee and Turner colour process 112
Legg, Stuart 85
Lenticular colour process 112
Le Prince, Louis 40
Le Roy, Jean Aimé 40
Liberty National Bank 85
**Liebeswaltzer** 102
Limbacher, James 114, 159
Loew, Marcus 131
Loew's 81–5, 131
Londe, Albert 40, 53
Loutherbourgh, Philip de 25
Lumière brothers 41, 45, 46, 50, 53, 56, 120

McDonagh colour system 114
McGuire, Frank 44
McHugh, John 131
**Madame Bertoldi, Contortionist** 50
Magic lantern 39, 52
Magnetic sound track 105, 126
Mamoulian, Rouben 147
Marey, Etienne Jules 34, 36, 37, 42, 53, 54
Massachusetts Institute of Technology 129, 140
Massole, Joseph 67
Master of ceremonies 92
Maxwell, James Clerk 29, 111, 112, 120
Maxwell, J. P. 71
**Meet Me in St Louis** 139
Megascope 11
Meliès, Georges 114, 120
**Melody Man, The** 133
**Mephisto** 123
Metro 131
Metropolitan and Bradford Trust 84, 87
Metz, Christian 1, 49, 56
**Mexican Knife Thrower** 50
Meyerstein 29
MGM 29
Microscope 29
**Mighty Joe Young** 119
**Milk White Flag** 50
**Miracle, The** 114
Mitchell, William D. 83
Moholy-Nagy, Laszlo 10
Monge, Gaspard 29
Morgan, J. P. 87
Morse, Samuel 21

**167**

Motion Picture Patents Company  49, 128
**Moulin Rouge**  151
Movietone  71, 74, 84
Moviola  88
Murillo, Bartolomé  147
Muybridge, Eadweard  33, 34, 36–8, 42, 54

National Provincial Bank  87
Natural Color Kinematograph Company  123
Nausorama  24
Neorama  24
Newton, Isaac  111
**Nice**  123
Niepce, Joseph Nicéphore  10, 20, 21, 32
Noiseograph  92
**No, No Nanette**  133

Octorama  24
**Oedipus Rex**  123
**Of Mice and Men**  119
O'Hara, Maureen  155
Olivier, Lawrence  148
Omniscope  32
**On With the Show**  101, 133
Ophthalmoscope  29
Optics  11, 12, 20, 28, 29, 56
Orthochromatic film stock  88
Orthophonic phonograph  71

Panochromatic film stock  88
Panorama  24, 26, 28
Paramount Pictures  80–3, 85
Parker, Alexander  43
Pasolini, Pier Paulo  159
Pathécolor  116, 117
Pathé Pictures  84, 116
Pathé-Nathan-Cinéromans  84, 87
Paul, Robert  49, 114
Persistence of vision  30–2
Perspective, monocular  12–14, 16–21, 28
    Ancient Classical  14
Peterson  68
Phakascope  29
Phantasmagoria  24, 25
Phénakistiscope  31–3, 37–9
Phi-phenomenon  30, 31
Phonoaction system  67
Phonofilm  68, 69
Phonograph  38, 42, 54, 63, 64
Photion  68
Photoelectric cell  67, 68, 70, 74–6
Photobioscope  31
Photographaphone  66
Photophone  82
Phototachyscope  40

Physionotrace  11
Physiorma  24
Pinel, Vincent  47
**Pinocchio**  139
Pioneer Films  136
**Pirate, The**  139
Pirenne, M. H.  18, 19
Plateau, Joseph  31, 32, 37, 39
Pleorama  24
Poccilorama  24
**Police Raid on an Opium Den**  50
Pollack, Peter  12, 13
Pomerade, George  64
Porta, Giovanni Battista della  12
**Portrait of Jenny**  119
Poulsen, Valdemar  68
Praxinoscope  31, 38, 40
Prescott, Barton  129
Prizmacolour  123–6, 132
Producers Distributing Corporation  82
Pronopiograph  11
Pross, John  48
Prudential Assurance  87
**Putting on the Ritz**  133

Quareograph  11

Radio Corporation of America (RCA)  74–6, 84, 85
Radio Engineering Company  75
Raff, Norman  44
**Rains Came, The**  119
**Ramona**  147
Rankine, A. O.  74
Ray, Man  10
RCA Photophone  75
**Rebel Without A Cause**  157
Rennahan, Ray  152, 153
Resnais, Alain  157
**Return of Frank James, The**  139
Reynaud, Emile  31, 40
**Rio Rita**  102, 133
RKO  82, 83, 119
**Robe, The**  144
Rockefeller  85, 87
Roget, Peter Mark  31
**Romeo and Juliet** (1953)  148
Rosolato, Guy  102
Rudge, John Arthur  40
Rühmer, Ernst  66
Ryan, R. T.  114

**Sandow in Feats of Strength**  50
Sanger-Shephard colour process  114
Schad, Christian  10
Scharf, Aaron  35
Scheele, C. W.  10
Schenck, Joseph  131
Schenck, Nicholas  131

Schott, Caspar  12
Schulze, J. H.  10
Selbeck  29
Selenium cell  67, 68
Sellers  32
Selznick, David O.  119, 136
Selznick International  136
**She Wore a Yellow Ribbon**  139, 157
Shields and Company  85
**Shoeshine and the Barber Shop**  50
**Show Boat** (1936)  101
**Show of Shows**  102
Siemens  83
**Sinbad the Sailor** (1947)  ??
Smith, Albert  48
Smith, G. A.  120, 121
**Song of the West**  133
Sonochrome dyes  118, 133
Soundograph  92
Sound head  70
Sound-on-disc  71–4, 93
Sound-on-film  62, 65–71, 74, 75, 93
Special effects  2
Spectroscope  29
Sponable, Earl  69, 70
Stampfer, Simon Ritter von  31
Stanley theatre chain  82
**Star is Born, A** (1937)  136
**Star Wars**  2
**State Fair** (1933)  139
Stencilling  116
Stéréofantascope  31, 32
Stereophonic sound  105
Sternberger, Dolf  26
Stroboscope  31, 32, 38
Stroheim, Erich von  148
Stuart and Halsey  85
Stull, William  132
**Sweet Flowers**  123

Tachyscope  31
Talbot, Henry Fox  9, 11, 20
Tate, A. O.  43
Technicolor  109, 120, 123, 124, 129
Technirama  144
Technirama-70  144
Telescope  29
Television  142–4
Thalofide cell  69
Thaumotrope  31
Théâtre Optique
**Thief of Baghdad, The** (1940)  139
**This is Cinerama**  114
3-D  126, 143, 145
**Three Little Pigs, The**  136
**Three Musketeers, The** (1921)  117
Tinting  117–20, 132, 157
**Toll of the Sea, The**  131
Tonbild Syndicate A. G. (Tobis)  83, 87

Tonfilm  68
Toning  117–20, 132, 157
**Tortilla Flat**  119
Toulouse-Lautrec, Henri de  151
Troland, Leonard  129
Tri-Ergon  67, 83, 87
TruColor  143
Tungsten lights  88
Tykociner, Joseph T.  67
Typorama  24
Tyrrell, Henry  56

United Artists (UA)  119
Udorama  24
UFA  83, 84
Universal  82, 85
Uranorama  24
Urban, Charles  120, 121, 123, 127, 128

Varley, Cornelius  11
Vinci, Leonardo da  13
VistaVision  144
Vitagraph  81
Vitaphone  70, 73
Vitascope  41, 48
Vogt, Hans  67

Walker, Alexander  79, 85
Wall, A. H.  23
W and F Film Service Ltd  84
Wardour Films  84
Warner Bros.  73, 79–83, 85
Warner Color  143
Warner, Harry  83
Warner, Samuel L.  73
**Waves and Spray**  122
Weaver, Eastman  129
**Wedding March, The**  148
Wente, E. C.  71
Werner, Anton von  26
Western Electric  70–6, 78, 79, 84, 85
**Western Union**  139
Westinghouse Electric and
    Manufacturing Company  74, 76
**What Price Glory?**  71
Wheatstone, Charles  31
**When Knighthood was in Flower**  117
**White Christmas**  144
Whitney, John  136
Widescreen  126, 140, 143
Williams, Alan  96
Williamson, James  120
**Wings**  76
Wireless Speciality Company  75
Wollaston, William Hyde  10, 29
Wollen, Peter  46, 48
Wong, Anna May  131
**World, the Flesh and the Devil, The**  123

Yale University 69
Young, Loretta 154
Young, Thomas 29, 31, 111

**Ziegfeld Follies** 139
**Ziegfeld Girl** 119

Zoechrome 123
Zoëtrope 31, 34
Zoogyroscope 40
Zoopraxiscope 34
Zukor, Adolph 83, 85

## British Film Institute Cinema Series
Edited by Ed Buscombe

The British Film Institute Cinema Series opens up a new area of cinema publishing with books that will appeal to people who are already interested in the cinema but want to know more, written in an accessible style by authors who have some authority in their field. The authors write about areas of the cinema where there is substantial popular interest, but as yet little serious writing, or they bring together for a wider audience some of the important ideas which have been developed in film studies in recent years.

Published:
Jane Feuer: **The Hollywood Musical**
Colin MacCabe: **Godard: Images, Sounds, Politics**
Steve Neale: **Cinema and Technology**

Forthcoming:
Pam Cook: **Feminism, Authorship and Cinema**
Richard Dyer: **The Stars**
Thomas Elsaesser: **New German Cinema**
Douglas Gomery: **The Golden Age of the Hollywood Studio 1925–50**
Maria Kornatowska: **Contemporary Polish Cinema**
Christopher Williams: **Film and Marxism**